MOTIVATING THOUGHTS OF MAHĀVĪRA

(Inspirations from the sacred Jaina texts)

Jainism is one of the ancient religions of India and an integral part of Indian culture. Lord Mahavira was the twenty-fourth Tirthankara of this religion. His sermons have been extensively documented in the Jain Agamas. His powerful teachings shed light on the philosophy of Jainism as well as on the moral and spiritual values for everyday life. His teachings about compassion and non-violence can be a major driving force in the present times. In today's world, which is ruled by the hunger for power and possessiveness, Mahavira's teachings need to be spread far and wide so that human beings may be inspired with humanity and humane values once again.

In this handy book 'Motivating Thoughts of Mahavira', Dulichand Jain presents a selection of some of the finest aphorisms from the ancient Jaina texts. For easy comprehension, he has divided the sutras into topics, such as knowledge and conduct, conquest of passions, doctrine of karma, reflection and intuition, learning, meditation and righteousness. He has given a simple title for every single aphorism along with the reference number. Its simple and lucid presentation will make it useful for the laypersons, students as well as scholars.

Dulichand Jain, an educationalist and social activist is the author of widely circulated books on Jain Philosophy and dictum : Jainvani ke moti (Hindi), Pearls of Jains Wisdom (English), Springs of Jaina Wisdom (English & Hindi), Universal Message of Lord Mahavira (English), Wisdom of Mahavira (English & Hindi), Main Mahavir Bol Raha Hoon (Hindi).

His articles are regularly published in leading magazines. A recipient of the 'Life Time Achievement Award' from the United Writers' Association in 1999, he has been honoured by World Jain Confederation, Mumbai in December 2013. He has also received a Hon. Doctorate in Philosophy from Washington University. He was invited by Federation of Jain Associations of North America to deliver two lectures at the Jaina Convention held in July 2001 at Chicago, USA. He is Chairman of Karuna International, Chennai; and also guides several reputed social cultural organization.

He was secretary of Research Foundation for Jainology and Jain Vidyashram at Chennai for fourteen years. He has received several eminent Awards.

Born on 1st November 1936, he lives with family at Chennai, India. He can be contacted at 09444047263; karunainternational@yahoo.co.in & dcj.chennai@gmail.com

MOTIVATING THOUGHTS OF MAHĀVĪRA

(Inspirations from the sacred Jaina texts)

Editor

Dulichand Jain 'Sahityaratna'

PRABHAT
PAPERBACKS

Published by
PRABHAT PAPERBACKS
4/19 Asaf Ali Road,
New Delhi-110 002 (INDIA)
e-mail: prabhatbooks@gmail.com

ISBN 978-93-5266-626-3
MOTIVATING THOUGHTS OF MAHĀVĪRA
Ed. Dulichand Jain 'Sahityaratna'

Edition
First, 2018

Publisher's Note

Among all the great personalities of the world, the name of Lord Mahavira is remembered with great reverence. He was the twenty-fourth Tirthankara of Jain religion. Millons of people have drawn inspiration from him and practised non-violence, compassion and vegetarianism. Mahatma Gandhi, the father of our nation, was highly influenced by his teachings.

Mahavira was born more than 2,500 years ago at Kundalpur in Vaishali Republic. The prevalence of superstitions, animal sacrifices, inhuman treatment of women and shudras awakened his revolutionary spirit. He decided to renounce the world and became a mendicant. He did penances for twelve -and-a-half long years and propagated the five values of non-violence, truth, non-stealing, chastity and non-possession.

Great personalities appear once in thousands of years but when they come to the earth, they prove to be a great boon to mankind. The path preached by Mahavira will guide mankind for all times to come.

This book is a compilation of select aphorisms of Lord Mahavira in a simple and reader-friendly format. It has also been published in Hindi by Prabhat Prakashan and is titled "Main Mahavir Bol Rahaa Hoon".

Contents

PART ONE

Life of Tīrthaṅkara Mahāvīra

Life of Tīrthaṅkara Mahāvīra

Inspiring Personality

Among all the great personalities of the world, the name of Lord Mahāvīra is remembered with great reverence. He was the twenty-fourth Tīrthaṅkara of Jaina religion. He was not the founder of this ancient religion which prevailed in India thousands of years before Pārsva and Mahāvīra, the last two Tīrthaṅkaras. Lord Ṛṣabhadeva was the first Tīrthaṅkara of Jainas. There are references to Ṛṣabha in Ṛgveda, Yajurveda and Bhāgavata Purāṇa. Lord Parśva, the twenty-third Tīrthaṅkara, lived and preached 250 years before Mahāvīra's advent.

The life of Lord Mahāvīra is very inspiring and thought-provoking. For the past 2500 years, millions of people have drawn inspiration from him and practised non-violence, vegetarianism and noble conduct. Even now, there are at least one crore followers of Mahāvīra in India. Mahatma Gandhi, the Father of the Nation, was highly influenced by his teachings. He applied the concept of Ahiṁsā and Satyāgraha at the national level successfully and was also victorious in getting these two principles universal recognition.

The Need for Revolution

India, the cradle of one of the ancient civilisations, witnessed enormous religious, political and social upheaval during this period. The prevalence of superstitions, animal sacrifices, inhuman treatment of women and śūdras awakened the revolutionary spirit in young Mahāvīra, then known as Vardhamāna. He studied deeply the adverse situations prevalent in the society at that time. His mind began to revolt and he wanted to find a solution for these problems. His parents were surprised to see his attitude and lifestyle remain unchanged even after his marriage. He kept aloof most of the times and was always absorbed in the Self. He had also decided to renounce the world and adopt the religious path. But at the insistence of his parents, he decided not to renounce the world as long as they were alive.

Desire for Renunciation

When Vardhamāna was 28 years old, his parents passed away. After some time, he sought the permission of his elder brother Nandīvardhana to renounce the world. But Nandīvardhana pleaded with him to delay the decision by a couple of years. Vardhamāna agreed. However, during the next two years, he led a simple and detached life. He was constantly absorbed in meditation. He observed the vow of celibacy, never ate at night, gave up anger and other passions and slept on the floor. His wife Yaśodā helped him in observing various religious practices. He also liberally donated gold coins and other items to the poor and the needy.

The Great Renunciation

At the age of thirty, Mahāvīra finally decided to renounce. As the news spread throughout the kingdom, the citizens flocked in thousands to bid him farewell. They were tear-filled and astounded that a prince who had everything at his command had decided to give it all up. King Nandīvardhana made magnificent arrangements for Vardhamāna's initiation. On the auspicious tenth of the dark half of mārgaśīrṣa month in 569 B.C., seated in a golden palanquin in a magnificent procession, Vardhamāna left his palace for the Jñātakhaṇḍa garden. King Nandīvardhana, his family, ministers and the entire public followed him with moist eyes. There, under an Aśoka tree, at the auspicious vijaya muhūrta, after fasting for two days, Vardhamāna removed his princely attire and ornaments, wore white robes and prepared himself for the initiation. Facing the eastward direction, he bowed to Siddhas, the liberated souls, and initiated himself in the holy order. He renounced all sinful activities of the past and vowed to remain equanimous throughout his life. He resolved to bear whatever hardships and afflictions he faced in the path and remain steadfast till he realised his final goal. The people gathered there bowed to Vardhamāna with deep reverence. And, thus, the prince of Kuṇḍagrāma became a śramaṇa (mendicant), determined to progress alone steadily on the path of perfection.

Path of Sādhanā

Vardhamāna, now called Mahāvīra because of the great vows he had taken as an ascetic, entered into a new phase of his life. He was free from attachment, affection and personal ties, without any worldly care and anxiety. They had no effect on him anymore. He could only see his goal of helping the people suffering from their miserable lot. He went on foot from one place to another, unmindful of hunger and thirst, cold and heat and rough and rugged pathways. He observed rigorous austerities for twelve-and-a-half long years until he achieved kevala-jñāna (omniscience).

Silent Sufferings

Śramaṇa Mahāvīra faced many adversities and calamities, brought upon him by natural and supernatural forces. It is difficult to find in history a personality who suffered such severe hardships as faced by Mahāvīra. He proved to be an incarnation of forbearance and forgiveness. The scriptures say: "Uggaṁ ca tavo kammaṁ visesao vaddhamāṇassa" (*Ā*va. Nir. 240), i.e., the austerities practised by Mahāvīra were more rigorous than the austerities practised by other Tīrthaṅkaras. His life was filled with equanimity, compassion and fearlessness. He mostly remained silent during this period.

Mention in Ācārāṅga Sūtra

We get a soul-stirring description of the rigorous austerities and spiritual practices of Śramaṇa Mahāvīra in the ninth chapter of the first part of Ācārā*ṇ*ga Sūtra. His direct disciple Gaṇadhara Sudharmāsvāmī has given a very vivid description of this period in it. It says that he was totally detached and equanimous in both favourable and unfavourable circumstances.

Brief excerpts of these spiritual practices are presented here:

Unclad Ascetic

When Mahāvīra renounced the world, he had only a piece of white cloth on his body. After thirteen months, this cloth got stuck while he was passing through some thorny bushes. Mahāvīra moved on, not bothering to retrieve it, and became an unclad ascetic. He calmly tolerated heat, cold, rain and other natural elemental forces, and even in severe cold, he meditated in open ground. When summer came, he exposed himself to the heat, squatting beneath the blazing sun.

Control of Food and Sleep

The venerable ascetic had great control over his body and mind. He lived on rough foods: rice, jujube and beans. On one occasion, only these sustained him for eight months. Sometimes he drank nothing for months. Even when he ate, his food was always of a tasteless kind. Sometimes he ate only on the third, fifteenth or thirtieth day of the month. Being free of desires, he remained engrossed in self-contemplation. He meditated without aversion or desire and was attached neither to sounds nor to colours. He was always alert and watchful in his austere life during his wanderings.

Renunciation of Attachment

Mahāvīra was not attached to sensual matters. Even when he suffered from some ailment, he did not take medication or rest. He always kept himself awake. He had an extraordinary control over his sleep and slept very little during this long period. He used to fix his concentration over a particular object and meditate for hours continuously.

Total Detachment

Mahāvīra always meditated in solitude and never mixed with people. He showed no interest in music, dance, drama or any other entertainment. When he was asked about his identity while wandering in secluded places, he gave a short reply: 'ahamaṁsi ti bhikkhuḥ', i.e., I am a Bhikshu (mendicant). He was dispassionate to the external world and was constantly engrossed in the contemplation of the self.

Mahāvīra wandered in search of Truth, ceasing to inflict injury on living beings and abandoning concern for the body. In some areas, Mahāvīra faced great adversities. In some villages, people did not allow him to stay overnight at their place. At other times, when he approached a village, the inhabitants met him outside and attacked him saying, 'get away from here'. In some places, he was beaten with sticks, fists and lances; he was hurt with clods and stones. Beating him again and again, such people raised a huge din.

Once when he sat in kāyotsarga (meditation), his body unmoving, some villagers cut his flesh, tore his hair and covered him with dirt. They picked him up and dropped him, disturbing his meditational postures. Absolutely not caring for the body, Mahāvīra bore all humiliations and pains ungrudgingly. Thus, the great ascetic proceeded on his path.

Non-violence and Compassion

Every moment of the ascetic life of Mahāvīra was devoted to the practice of non-violence and compassion. When he went from door to door begging for alms, he always cared that no person, animal or bird was disturbed. He avoided those houses where some other ascetics, Brāhmaṇas or other persons stood begging for alms so as not to disturb their livelihood. He never gave a chance to foster hatred, enmity or aversion to anybody.

"With supreme knowledge, supreme intuition, supreme conduct, supreme uprightness, supreme valour, supreme dexterity, supreme patience, supreme contentment and supreme insight, the Venerable One meditated for twelve-and-a-half years in self-contemplation and proceeded on the supreme path to that final liberation which is the fruit of truthfulness, restraint and good conduct." (Kalpa Sūtra, 120)

Mahāvīra spent his whole time deeply thinking about the goal of human life and its problems. He contemplated upon crucial philosophical and metaphysical solutions to problems confronting the people at that time.

Nails in the Ears

During the thirteenth year, Śramaṇa Mahāvīra was meditating on the outskirts of Chamāṇi village. At that time, a shepherd came there with oxen and instructed him to look after them till he returned in the evening. Mahāvīra was in deep meditation and, hence, did not reply. When the shepherd returned in the evening, he did not find the oxen there as they had wandered away. He asked Mahāvīra about the whereabouts of his oxen, but he was still in meditation and did not give any reply. The shepherd became furious and decided to punish him. He collected two sharp sticks from the forest and hammered them into Mahāvīra's ears. Mahāvīra did not utter a single word through the painful incident and continued meditating. After completing his meditation, he proceeded towards the house of a merchant named Siddhartha in Madhyamā city for begging alms. The merchant noticed nails in the ears of the great ascetic and was deeply saddened. With tears filled in his eyes, he called a reputed Vaidya named Kharaka, who removed the nails and applied some oil to heal the wound.

This was almost the last of all adversities that Śramaṇa Mahāvīra faced when observing spiritual practices for twelve-and-a-half long years (Triṣ*aṣṭiś*alākapuruṣacaritra, 10.4)

Life as a Tīrthaṅkara

After attaining omniscience, Bhagāvan Mahāvīra began to preach and give sermons, wandering from one place to another on foot. From Jambhiyagrāma, he went to

Madhyama Pāvāpurī. At the place, a large religious sacrifice had been organised by a Brahmin named Somila. Several reputed scholars and their disciples had assembled to take part in the sacrifice. Most prominent among them was Indrabhūti Gautama.

These Brahmins heard the news of Mahāvīra having attained the omniscient state. But they did not believe it. So, they came to the place where Mahāvīra was giving his sermon. Indrabhūti was a great scholar, well versed in the Vedas, and he felt that there cannot be a higher scholar than him in the whole world. He wanted to defeat Mahāvīra. However, when he reached the assembly hall and saw Mahāvīra, all his pride and vanity disappeared.

On seeing him, Mahāvīra addressed him, "O Indrabhūti, you have doubts about the self." Indrabhūti was surprised because he had not yet uttered a word about it. It was true that he had doubts in his mind about the existence of the soul. Mahāvīra said, "The soul is self-evident (pratyakṣa) and no proof would be needed to demonstrate the existence of it either through sense experience or through reasoning. The fundamental principle 'I think' leads to the establishment of the self. The very fact that I am aware of my experiences, like doubting and memory, leads to the establishment of this fundamental truth. The Jīva (self) is different from the body. The Jīva is characterised by consciousness (upayoga) while the body is unconscious (jada)."

He further explained the distinction between pure self (ātman) and empirical self (bahirātman), "The self is pure and perfect, it is eternal and indestructible." He then explained the six substances that constitute the universe, the five great vows, twelve reflections, etc. All of Indrabhūti's doubts were cleared. He became a disciple of Mahāvīra and joined the ascetic order with his disciples.

All Doubts Cleared

Indrabhūti was followed by ten other very eminent scholars. Although they all were well versed in the Vedic scriptures, each one of them had some doubt. Even before they could disclose their doubts, Mahāvīra revealed it to them and gave convincing replies. Here are the details of the doubts which were lingering in the minds of these scholars:

Indrabhūti: about the existence of the soul.

Agnibhūti: about Karmas.

Vāyubhūti: whether the soul and body are one or different.

Vyakta: about substances, such as earth, air, fire, etc.

Sudharmā: about reincarnation.

Manditputra: about bondage and liberation.

Mauryaputra: about heaven and heavenly bodies.

Akampita: about the existence of hell.

Acalabhrātā: about meritorious and demeritorious deeds.

Metārya: about rebirth.

Prabhava: about emancipation.

The Early Initiation

Lord Mahāvīra convincingly cleared the doubts of all the above scholars. They were all fully satisfied and took initiation along with each of their 400 followers. Thus, on the very first day of his sermon, 4,411 persons became his disciples. This incident of the initiation of such a large number of scholars in a single day reached far and wide and thousands of men and women came to listen to his discourses. It included rich and poor, kings and their ministers, merchants, farmers, craftsmen and all classes of people. Many became his disciples and followers.

Composition of Aṅgas and Pūrvas

The eleven eminent Brahmins became the eleven Gaṇadharas. Indrabhūti Gautama became the prime disciple of Lord Mahāvīra. With his vast knowledge of the Vedas in the background, he could master transcendental knowledge. The twelve Aṅgas and fourteen Pūrvas were composed. His brothers Agnibhūti and Vayubhūti mastered the Aṅgas and Pūrvas. After mastering the teachings of Mahāvīra, the eleven Gaṇadharas formed the nucleus of the new order. They composed all scriptural literature and rules of conduct, and afterwards narrated the sacred literature to the other disciples.

In the Saṅgha established by Lord Mahāvīra, there was no difference between men and women. Both were regarded equally. Women were also initiated as nuns which was a great revolutionary step at that time.

Spread of Jaina Religion

Soon the Jaina order grew to a large number of 14,000 monks, 36,000 nuns, 1,59,000 laymen and 3,18,000 laywomen. The monks and nuns had to follow strict rules of conduct. They were to follow the five great vows and be obedient to the teacher and the head of the order. The conduct of monks and nuns was regulated down to the minutest details – begging of alms, respecting the preceptor, taking medical treatment; residence, their duty at the time of calamity or lawlessness in the country... The householders were to follow the primary vows (Aṇuvratas). They served the ascetics by offering alms, providing a temporary dwelling and propagating the cause of religion. The formation of the four-fold order based on strict discipline certainly helped in its survival.

Onward March

For thirty long years, Lord Mahāvīra went around preaching the religion of Ahiṁsa and Anekānta (Non-absolutism). He visited important places, such as Kāśī, Kośala, Vatsa, Campā, Pāñcāla, Magadha, Rājagṛha, Aṅga, Baṅga, Kaliṅga and many others. Those who heard his teachings were inspired by the pure and perfect words of the Master. The Jaina canonical works and texts, such as Bhagavatī, Aupāpatika, Harivaṁśa Purāṇa and a host of others have given graphic description of wanderings of Mahāvīra and the benefit that the people derived from his noble teachings.

Śreṇika Bimbisāra, the king of Magadha, became his follower. Earlier, he was a follower of Lord Buddha. His queen Celanā was a great devotee of Mahāvīra. We find a vivid description of the dialogue held between Bimbisāra and Anāthīmuni (a monk) in Uttarārādhyayana Sūtra, which inspired the king to become a follower of Mahāvīra. Several incidents about his wit and wisdom are narrated in Jaina texts.

Cetaka, the head of Vaiśālī republic and maternal grandfather of Mahāvīra, also had great faith in his teachings. He took oath of the twelve vratas to be observed by a householder. He contributed greatly in spreading Jaina religion far and wide. Many kings, such as Vīrāngada, Vīrayaśa, Sañjaya, Eṇeyaka, Seya, Śiva, Udrāyaṇa and Śaṅkha-Kaśīvardhana joined his order and became patrons of this religion.

The Saṅgha established by Mahāvīra was well organized and disciplined. Perhaps it is because of the severity of discipline and clinging to the original tradition that the Jaina order has not swelled in number but has remained steady in India.

Mahā-Nirvāṇa

Mahāvīra was now seventy-two years old. At the last lap of his journey, he came to Pāvā and stayed in the garden of Rājā Hastipāla. He gave several discourses which were recorded in Uttarārādhyayana Sūtra. He sat for his last meditation on a slab of stone. It was in the early hours of the fifteenth day of the dark fortnight of Kārtika month when he attained the state of Nirvāṇa in 527 B.C. At that time, only two of the eleven Gaṇadharas, Indrabhūti and Sudharmāsvāmi, were alive while the others had attained Nirvāṇa earlier. Indrabhūti Gautama attained omniscience a few hours after his great Master passed away. These two events are even now celebrated by Jains during the festival of Dīpāvalī (festival of lights) - a tradition started by the local kings on that very day. As the Kalpa Sūtra says:

"On that night, when the venerable ascetic Mahāvīra attained Nirvāṇa cutting asunder the ties of birth, old age and death, became a Siddha, thus finally liberated.... His oldest disciple, the Monk Indrabhūti of the Gautama gotra, obtained the highest knowledge and intuition, called Kevala, which is infinite, supreme and full." (Kalpa Sūtra, 126)

"And on that night during which the venerable Ascetic Mahāvīra obtained Nirvāṇa, the eighteen confederate kings of Kāśī and Kośala, the Mallas and Licchavīs instituted an illumination with lighted lamps and stated, 'Since the internal (bhāva) light (of intelligence) is gone, let us make an illumination with the external (dravya) light (of matter)'." (Kalpa Sūtra, 127)

Great personalities appear once in thousands of years, but when they come to the earth, they prove to be a great boon to mankind. The life and teachings of Lord Mahāvīra have inspired millions of people to embrace the noble path preached by him. The three principles of Ahiṁsā (non-violence), Anekānta (non-absolutism) and Aparigraha (non-possession) will guide mankind for all time to come.

□

PART TWO

A Selection of Inspiring Aphorisms from the Jaina Scriptures

I
Prayer

1. NAMASKĀRA MANTRA (The Five-Fold Obeisance)

The Namaskāra Mantra, also known as Navkār Mantra, is the basic mantra of Jainism.

It is a universal mantra because it does not refer to any specific God or Goddess. By reciting it, we worship all the spiritually evolved beings in this universe so that we can internalise their great and noble qualities.

In the first part, we bow down to the Arihantas (those who have conquered inner passions and desires), Siddhas (liberated souls), Āchāryas (heads of religious sects), Upādhyāyas (spiritual teachers), and all the Sadhus (monks and nuns).

The second half of this mantra states that with this five-fold salutation, we cleanse ourselves of all sins. Hence, it is the most auspicious among all mantras.

1. The five-fold obeisance is given below:
   (Namaskāra Mantra)
   Obeisance to the Victors (Arihantas)
   Obeisance to the Liberated Souls (Siddhas)
   Obeisance to the Preceptors (Āchāryas)
   Obeisance to the Spiritual Teachers (Upādhyāyas)
   Obeisance to all the Saints (Sādhus) in the world.

This sublime five-fold obeisance (Namaskāra Mantra) destroys all the sins and is supremely auspicious.

– Āvaśyaka Sūtra 1.2

2. Auspicious are the Arihantas, Siddhas, Sādhus and the code of conduct (dharma) preached by them.

   – *Āvaśyaka Sūtra 4.1*

3. Namaskāra Mahāmantra is the supreme mantra, which bestows all that is auspicious and worthy; it also liberates the soul from the worldly sojourn. The chanting of the mantra itself brings peace and joy.

   – *Kām. Kath. 154*

□

II
Self

2. PRECEPTS ON THE SELF

Nature of the Soul

1. My own soul is the river Vaitaraṇī (a river in hell) and the thorny tree of Śālmali. It is also the miraculous cow Kāmadhenu and the divine garden Nandana.

   – *Uttarā. Sū. 20.36*

Friend and Foe

2. The soul is the begetter of both happiness and sorrow; it is its own friend when it treads the path of righteousness and is its own enemy when it treads the forbidden path.

   – *Uttarā. Sū. 20.37*

No Difference

3. Essentially there is no difference between the souls, be it the soul of an elephant or of an ant.

   – *Bha. Sū. 7.8*

Self-Purification

4. One who is free of deceit is pure, and once he is pure, dharma abides in him. It is only the pure who attain emancipation like the sparkling fire sprinkled with ghee.

   – *Uttarā. Sū. 3.12*

The Shrine of the Soul

5. Religion is the pond; celibacy is its sacred shrine (ghāṭa). It is full of tranquillity and placid with the serene thought process of the soul. Having made ablution there, I become pure, clean, thoroughly cooled and devoid of impurity.

– Uttarā. Sū. 12.46

The Knower

6. The soul is the knower and the knower is the soul. Through knowledge, the soul comprehends itself as well as the external world. This attribute of knowing is exclusive to the soul.

– Ācā Sū. 2.5.5.104-105

Abode of Excellence

7. Know for certain that the soul (jīva) is the abode of excellent virtues, the best among the substances and supreme among the realities.

– Dvā. Anu. 204

Kinds of Souls

8. Souls (jīvas) are of three kinds – external, internal and supreme. The supreme soul is of two kinds: (i) enlightened (arihanta); and (ii) liberated (siddha).

– Mo. Pā. 4

The Three Souls

9. External soul is that which is led by the senses. Internal soul is that which knows itself to be different from the body. Supreme soul is that which has annihilated the karmas and attained liberation.

– Mo. Pā. 5

The Pure Soul

10. The pure soul is free from the activities of mind, body and speech. It is free from conflict, is detached, formless, without substratum, dispassionate, unblemished, and free from delusion and fear.

– Ni.Sā. 43

No Deficiencies

11. The pure soul is free from complexities, attachment, blemishes, desire, anger, pride, ego and all kinds of deficiencies.

–Ni.Sā. 44

3. Self-Conquest

Fight with Self

1. Fight with your own self; what is the use of fighting with the external foes? Difficult it is to conquer your own self.

– Uttarā. Sū. 9.35

Conquer Your Self

2. Oh man! You are your own friend, why do you seek the company of other friends? Control and conquer your own self. By doing so, you will be liberated from all miseries and sorrows.

– Ācā Sū. 1.3.3.64

Greatest Victory

3. Victory over one's self is greater than conquering thousands and thousands of enemies on the attlefield. A true conqueror is one who conquers his own self.

– Uttarā. Sū. 9.34

The True Conquest

4. Fight with your own self, what will you gain by fighting external foes? One who conquers one's own self alone experiences supreme bliss.

– Ācā Sū. 1-5.3, 45-46

The Conquered Soul

5. One must conquer one's own self, for difficult it is to conquer it. One who does so is fortunate in this world and will be so in the next.

– Uttarā. Sū. 1.15

4. Introspection

Contemplate on Supreme Soul

1. Jina urges one to repudiate the external soul through mind, speech and deed, absorb oneself in the internal soul and contemplate the supreme soul.

– Mo. Pā. 7

Beyond Body and Mind

2. The soul is neither the body nor the mind, neither the speech nor their cause. It is also neither the doer, nor the cause of action, nor the approver of any action.

– Pra.Sā. 2.68

Destroy all Modifications

3. I am alone, pure, free from attachment and full of infinite knowledge and perception. Firmly established in the self, I destroy all those modifications which are alien to me.

– Sa.Sā. 73

Knowing the Self

4. How shall one know the self? By discerning the self to be distinct from the body shall one be able to know the self.

– Sa.Sā. 296

External Adjuncts

5. My soul, endowed with knowledge and vision, is alone eternally mine; all others are alien to me and are in the nature of external adjuncts.

– Bha.Pā. 59

Realisation of Soul

6. It is very difficult to realise the soul. Only with sufferings is the soul realised.

– Mo. Pā. 65

Greater Consistency

7. When the water becomes clearer, one is able to view the reflection with greater clarity. So also, when the

self becomes inspired to know the reality, one starts acquiring knowledge with greater consistency.

– Āva. Ni. 1169

Distinct from Body

8. When the inflow of karmas through the three channels of mind, speech and body is completely stopped, the soul realises itself to be distinct from the body.

– Uttarā. Cū. 1

Introspection

9. At the end of the day, an awakened person contemplates thus - what noble deeds have I done and what have I not done? What good deeds remain to be done which I could have, but have not accomplished?

– Daśa. Cū. 2.12

Experience Lightness

10. Just as a person burdened by a load experiences relief when he unburdens the load, an aspirant, by reviewing his wrong deeds and confessing them before his spiritual guide, experiences lightness.

– O. Ni. 806

Dreadful Temptations

11. The dreadful tree of desires brings forth dreadful fruits; this tree being permanently uprooted, O great sage, I wander peacefully.

– Uttarā.Sū.23.48

Soul Different from Body

12. Know the soul to be different from the perishable body and steadily engage yourself in destroying the karmic influence.

– Ācā Sū. 1.4.3

Conquering all Enemies

13. On conquering one, I have conquered five; on conquering five, I have conquered ten; by this ten-fold victory, I have conquered all enemies.

– Uttarā. Sū. 23.36

Ten Powerful Enemies

14. One's unconquered mind together with four passions and five uncontrolled senses are the ten powerful enemies of man. Conquering these ten, O great sage, I move about righteously.

– Uttarā.Sū.23.38

5. Self-Restraint

Spiritual Exertion

1. Just as a tortoise draws its limbs into its own shell, a wise man should withdraw his senses from evil by spiritual exertion.

– Sū. Kr. Sū. 1.8.16

Desist from Wrong Deeds

2. When a wrong deed is committed consciously or otherwise, the aspirant should immediately desist from that and never repeat it.

– Daśa. Sū. 8.31

Overcome Sensual Pleasures

3. Just as a horse can be controlled by a bridle, the sensual pleasures and passions can be overcome by knowledge, meditation and power of penance.

– Ma.Sa. 621

Discipline the Self

4. How can one discipline others, when one is unable to discipline one's own self?

– Sū.Kṛ. Sū. 1.1.2.17

Continence

5. Continence is four-fold - mind, body, speech and possessions.

– Sthā.Sū. 4.2

Controlled Sense Organs

6. A well-controlled horse that gallops fast reaches his destination safely; so also the sense organs well

controlled by the reins of scriptural knowledge are beneficial in realising the self.

– *Ma.Sa. 622*

Need for Restraint

7. The unprotected and unrestrained soul wanders aimlessly in the worldly sojourn; the careful and restrained soul is liberated from all miseries. Knowing this, protect your Self by controlling the senses.

– *Daśa. Cū. 2.16*

Withdraw from Misdeeds

8. Whenever a wise man notices that he is deviating from the path of righteousness in thought, word or deed, he should immediately withdraw himself from that misdeed like a horse controlled by tightened reins.

– *Daśa. Sū. 2.14*

Observe Austerity

9. Destroy the passions by observing austerity and also relinquish the tendency of enjoying the sensual pleasures.

– *Ācā. Sū. 1.4.3*

Control the Desires

10. It is better to control myself through self-restraint and austerity than being enslaved and subjugated by others.

– *Uttarā.Sū.1.16*

Ten Mighty Enemies

11. The five senses, the four passions, i.e., anger, pride, deceit and greed, and the unconquered self are the ten mighty enemies; when the self is conquered, everything is conquered.

– *Uttarā.Sū.9.36*

□

III
Precepts on Knowledge and Conduct

6. Right Faith

The Pathway to Liberation

1. Belief in the existence of six entities (dravya) such as dharma is right faith; understanding Aṅgas and Pūrvas is right knowledge; and the practice of austerity is right conduct. These three constitute the pathway to liberation as understood from the practical viewpoint.

– Pañcā.160

Nine Aspects of Reality

2. The nine aspects of reality (nav tattva) are: living being (jīvā), non-living being (ajīvā), binding of the soul by karma (bandha), merit (puṇya), demerit (pāpa), inflow of karma (āṣrava), stoppage of karma (saṁvara), annihilation of karma (nirjarā), and emancipation (mokṣa).

– Uttarā.Sū.28.14

Right Belief

3. He who verily believes in the existence of the nine aspects of reality possesses righteousness. This is acquired by one's own discrimination of right and wrong or by following the teachings of the preceptor.

– Uttarā.Sū.28.15

Attaining Purity

4. With knowledge one understands the nature of the substances; with faith, one believes in them; with conduct, one puts an end to the flow of karmas; and with austerity, one attains purity.

– Uttarā.Sū.28.35

Liberation

5. Without (right) faith, there is no (right) knowledge; without (right) knowledge, there is no virtuous conduct; without virtues, there is no annihilation of karmas; and without annihilation, there is no liberation.

– Uttarā.Sū.28.30

Right Vision

6. When one is completely engrossed in the contemplation of the self, he is said to have right vision.

– Bhā. Pā. 31

Knowledge and Conduct

7. Right knowledge is of no use in the absence of right conduct and conduct is of no use in the absence of right knowledge. When a lame man and a blind man in a forest are caught in a conflagration, both get burnt because the lame cannot walk and the blind cannot see.

– Āva. Ni. 102

Harmony

8. The desired result is attained when there is harmony between right knowledge and right conduct, for a chariot does not move by one wheel alone. In a forest conflagration, when a blind and a lame help each other, both manage to reach the destination safely.

– Āva. Ni. 102

A Person of Right Faith

9. If a person has even an iota of attachment, then the mastery of all the scriptures cannot beget him

knowledge of the soul. When he does not know the soul, how can he know the other substances? When he knows neither the soul nor the other substances, how can he be a person of right faith?

– Sa.Sā. 201-202

Defiled Persons

10. Those who do not possess right faith are defiled persons. There is no liberation for the persons devoid of right faith. Those who have given up right conduct (but have right faith) may attain liberation by practising right conduct again, but there is no hope for those who do not have right faith.

– Bhā. Pā. 66

The Value of Right Faith

11. The value of right faith is much greater than possessing all the treasures of the three worlds.

– Bha. Ā.741

Righteousness

12. The basis of Righteousness (dharma) is faith.

– Da. Pā. 2

Unfit for Worship

13. A person devoid of faith is unfit for adoration and worship.

– Da. Pā. 2

Who Has Right Faith?

14. A person having right faith is one who knows what is to be relinquished and what is to be accomplished.

– Sū. Pā. 5

Devoid of Righteousness

15. If a person devoid of righteousness undertakes severe austerities for thousands of years, still he will be unable to achieve self-realisation.

– Da. Pā. 5

7. Right Knowledge

Right Knowledge

1. The most important thing in life is knowledge. Knowledge precedes compassion. All noble people take this into account. How will an ignorant person distinguish the meritorious deeds from the evil ones?

– Daśa. Sū. 4.10

Self-Restraint

2. How can an aspirant who does not know the nature of the living and the non-living substances, thus being ignorant of both, practise self-restraint?

– Daśa. Sū. 4.12

Kinds of Knowledge

3. Knowledge is of five kinds: (i) Scriptural (sruta-jñāna), (ii) Knowledge derived through the five senses and the mind (mati-jñāna), (iii) Clairvoyance (avadhi-jñāna), (iv) Telepathy (manaḥ-paryaya jñāna), and (v) Omniscience (kevala- jñāna).

– Uttarā.Sū.28.4

Acquisition of Knowledge

4. Perfect meditation, which annihilates all karmas, is attained through knowledge. By annihilating the karmas, a person becomes liberated. Hence, one should engage constantly in the acquisition of knowledge.

– Ra. Sā. 138

Righteous Person

5. As is the nature of the lotus leaf to remain untouched by water, so does a righteous person remain fully unaffected by passions and sensual pleasures.

– Bā. Pā. 154

Sacred Knowledge

6. Just as a threaded needle does not get lost even when it falls in a heap of rubbish, so a person

endowed with sacred knowledge does not get lost in worldly sojourn.

– Uttarā.Sū.29.60

Master of Scriptures

7. He who knows the self to be wholly different from the impure body and comprehends it to be the knower of all substances is said to be a master of all scriptures.

– Kā. A. 465

Supreme Knowledge

8. From the point of view of spiritual practice, knowledge of scriptures is the supreme knowledge.

– Uttarā.Cū. 1

Goad of Knowledge

9. The vitiated mind is like a furious elephant, but can be controlled by the goad of right knowledge.

– Bha. Ā.760

What is Knowledge?

10. According to the teachings of Jina, knowledge helps understand the truth, controls the mind and purifies the soul.

– Mū. 267

Comprehensive Reach

11. The light of knowledge is true and supreme, for nothing can obstruct its path. When compared to the sunlight, its reach is comprehensive.

– Arh. Pra. 19.47

The Beneficial Path

12. After listening to scriptures, a person knows the difference between good and evil deeds. Having known both, he should practise that which is conducive to reach the highest goal.

– Daśa. Sū. 4.11

8. Right Conduct

Liberation

1. Without (right) faith, there is no (right) knowledge; without (right) knowledge, there is no virtuous conduct; without virtues, there is no annihilation of karmas; and without annihilation, there is no liberation.

– Uttarā.Sū.28.30

Characterless Person

2. As the light from crores of burning lamps is of no avail to a blind person, so also the study of numerous scriptures is of no use to a person who has no character.

– Āva. Ni. 98

Inner Eye

3. Even limited knowledge of scriptures is beneficial to a person whose inner eye has opened just as the light of even one lamp is sufficient to show the path to a person whose eyes are open.

– Āva. Ni. 99

Detachment

4. A person who is detached does not enjoy sensual pleasures though externally he may seem to be doing so. On the other hand, a person may not be sensuously experiencing them but suffers due to attachment with them. A person acting in a drama does not, in fact, become transformed into that character.

– Adh. Sā. 5.25

Treading the Path of Liberation

5. A person who knows swimming but does not swim when he falls in water ultimately drowns. So also a person who knows the path of liberation but does not tread it fails to cross the worldly sojourn.

– Uttarā.Sū.28.30

Virtuous Conduct

6. Even a little knowledge will yield great fruit if it is accompanied by virtuous conduct.

– Śī. Pā. 6

Character is Important

7. Without character, human birth is futile.

– Śī. Pā. 19

Noble Conduct

8. Noble conduct includes compassion, self-control, truth, non-stealing, celibacy, contentment, right faith, knowledge and austerity.

– Śī. Pā. 19

Right Conduct

9. Renunciation of sensual pleasures is right conduct.

– Śī. Pā. 40

Self-Restraint

10. Some householders are superior to certain monks (who falter) in self-control, but the self-restrained monks are superior to all householders.

– Uttarā.Sū.5.20

Sinful Ascetic

11. The garb of an ascetic, lion skin, nakedness, matted hair, tonsured head and other external manifestations do not save a sinful ascetic.

– Uttarā.Sū.5.21

9. The Right World View

Universe and Non-Universe

1. Do not believe that the universe (loka) and non-universe (aloka) do not exist, but believe that they do exist.

– Sū.Kṛ. Sū. 2.5.12

Souls and Non-Souls

2. Do not believe that souls and non-souls do not exist, but believe that they do exist.

– Sū.Kṛ. Sū. 2.5.13

Medium of Motion and Rest

3. Do not believe that medium of motion (dharma) and medium of rest (adharma) do not exist, but believe that they do exist.

   – *Sū.Kṛ. Sū.* 2.5.14

Bondage and Liberation

4. Do not believe that bondage and liberation do not exist, but believe that they do exist.

   – *Sū.Kṛ. Sū.* 2.5.15

Inflow and Stoppage of Karma

5. Do not believe that there are no inflow and stoppage of karma, but believe that they do exist.

   – *Sū.Kṛ. Sū.* 2.5.17

Karmas and their Annihilation

6. Do not believe that experiencing the effect of karmas and their annihilation do not exist, but believe that they do exist.

   – *Sū.Kṛ. Sū.* 2.5.18

Attachment and Aversion

7. Do not believe that there is no attachment and aversion, but believe that they do exist.

   – *Sū.Kṛ. Sū.* 2.5.22

Four-Fold Existence

8. Do not believe that the four-fold existence of births does not exist, but believe that it does exist.

   – *Sū.Kṛ. Sū.* 2.5.23

Liberation and Non-Liberation

9. Do not believe that neither there is liberation nor non-liberation, but believe that they do exist.

   – *Sū.Kṛ. Sū.* 2.5.25

Liberated Souls

10. Do not believe that there is no abode of liberated souls, but believe that it does exist.

    – *Sū.Kṛ. Sū.* 2.5.26

10. Four Things Difficult to Obtain

Rare Achievement

1. Rare it is for living beings to obtain four things of paramount value: human birth, listening to the holy scriptures, to have faith in them and endeavour to practise self-restraint.

   – *Uttarā.Sū.3.1*

Actions Determine Destiny

2. Sometimes the living being goes to heaven, sometimes to hell and sometimes becomes a demon in accordance with his or her karmas.

   – *Uttarā.Sū.3.3*

Listening to Scriptures

3. Even after obtaining a human body, difficult it is to listen to the holy scriptures and thereafter practise austerity, forgiveness and non-violence.

   – *Uttarā.Sū.3.8*

Faith

4. Even after listening to the holy scriptures, it is extremely difficult to cultivate faith in them because many people, despite knowing the right path, still go astray.

   – *Uttarā.Sū.3.9*

Exertion

5. Even after listening to the holy scriptures, and believing them, it is difficult to tread the path of righteousness because many people have faith in religion but do not practise it.

   – *Uttarā.Sū.3.10*

Victory over Karmas

6. Being born as a human being, believing in religion and following it meticulously, an ascetic should practise self-restraint and annihilate the karmas completely.

   – *Uttarā.Sū.3.11*

Repentance

7. He who does not endeavour to tread the path of righteousness in this birth repents at the time of death.

– Āva. Ni. 837

Unworthy Person

8. A person who carelessly wastes human life, which is most difficult to acquire and which is transient like the flash of lightning, is unworthy and not a noble person.

– Āva. Ni. 841

Superior Ascetics

9. Ascetics who are always absorbed in the contemplation of the self and who sincerely pursue knowledge, faith, conduct and humility are superior to others. They are the supreme lotuses of this pond-like universe.

– Sū.K□. Ni. 156

11. Path of Liberation

Path of Liberation

1. Faith, knowledge and conduct together constitute the path of liberation; this is the path to be followed. The saints have averred that if this is followed in the right way, it will lead to liberation; otherwise it will lead to bondage.

– Pañcā.164

Unfit for Liberation

2. One unfit for liberation (abhavya) may develop faith and have knowledge of the religion, show some liking for it and perform it. But all this he does to attain some worldly pleasure and not to annihilate the karmas.

– Adh. Sā. 12.4

Path of Liberation

3. Knowledge, faith, conduct and austerity together constitute the pathway of liberation as told by the Omniscient who possess perfect knowledge.

– Uttarā.Sū. 28.2

Detachment

4. He who has detached himself from sensual pleasure liberates himself soon from the worldly sojourn.

– Āva. Ni. 177

Emancipation

5. Knowledge enables one to know the truth; austerity enables one to purify the soul; and self-restraint enables one to give up the forbidden deeds. It is the declaration of Jaina dharma that the accomplishment of the above three in their entirety leads to emancipation.

– Āva. Ni. 103

Renouncing Pleasures

6. A person who renounces worldly pleasures, although he is capable of enjoying them, destroys the great heaps of karmas, which ultimately yields the fruit of emancipation.

– Bha. Sū. 7.149

Powerful Self

7. I have heard and experienced that bondage and liberation are within your Self.

– Ācā. Sū. 1.5.2.36

□

IV
Precepts on Fundamentals

12. Knowledge of Fundamentals

Soul's Characteristics

1. A soul is characterised by consciousness, is eternal, immortal, formless, different from the body, and the doer and enjoyer of all its actions.

– Dhyāna. 55

Non-Soul

2. Saints call that as non-soul (ajīvā) which does not have any knowledge of pleasure or pain, cannot identify what is beneficial and does not fear that which is detrimental.

– Pañcā.125

Kinds of Non-Soul

3. Ajīvā (non-soul) is of five kinds: Matter (pudgala), medium of motion (dharma), medium of rest (adharma), space (ākāśa), and time (kāla). Among these, matter alone has form as it has the attributes of colour, etc.; the rest of them are formless.

– Dravya. 15

Cause of Bondage

4. The soul is imperceptible to the senses as it is formless; because it possesses no corporeal form, it is eternal. However, attachment and such other imperfections cause bondage, and this bondage is the cause of worldly existence.

– Uttarā. Sū. 14.19

Bondage of Souls

5. Due to attachment, karma binds the soul; a soul which is free from attachment becomes liberated from karmas. This in brief is the concept of bondage of souls.

– Pra. Sā. 2.87

Desirous of Emancipation

6. One desirous of emancipation should not have even an iota of attachment. By conquering all attachments, one crosses the ocean of worldly existence.

– Pañcā.172

Characteristics of Substances

7. All substances have existence and are characterised by origination, cessation and persistence.

– Pañcā.10

Free from Bondage

8. A true aspirant must ponder thus: "O Lord, what entangles a soul and sinks it into karmic bondage? How can a soul rise from its bondage and move towards liberation?"

– Jñātā. 1/6/4

Eighteen Sins

9. (i) Violence, (ii) untruth, (iii) theft, (iv) carnal desire, (v) possessiveness, (vi) anger, (vii) conceit, (viii) deceit, (ix) greed, (x) attachment, (ix) aversion, (xii) engaging in quarrels, (xiii) speaking ill of others, (xiv) gossiping, (xv) indulging in sensual pleasures without restraint, (xvi) malevolent criticism, (xvii) deceiving, and (xviii) wrong faith are the eighteen types of sins that bind the soul and drag him to lower existences. When one renounces the eighteen types of sins, he is able to annihilate all his karmas and attain emancipation.

– Jñātā. 1/6/8

□

V

Precepts on Conquest of Passions

13. Anger

Anger

1. Intense anger that lasts forever like a deep crack on a rock drags the soul to hellish existence.

   – Sthā. Sū. 4.2

Declining of Character

2. When anger and other passions get more and more inflamed, character begins to decline lower and lower.

   – Ni. Bhā. 2790

Blinded by Anger

3. A person blinded by anger does not hesitate to kill his mother, sister and even his children.

   – Vasu. Śrā. 67

Symptoms of Anger

4. A person overcome by anger turns pale, loses all charm and becomes restless. Even under favourable circumstances, he feels uneasy and trembles as though he is under the influence of an evil spirit.

   – Bha. Ārā.1360

The Effects of Anger

5. Anger is favourable to the enemy. It brings grief to the person (who gets angry) and to his relatives. Anger results in defeating the person (who is angry) and ultimately destroys him.

   – Bha. Ārā.1365

Anger is Destructive

6. Just as a spark of fire destroys the year-long accumulated stock of grains, so also the fire of anger destroys all the divine qualities of a monk.

– Bha. Ārā.1367

Destruction of Love

7. Anger spoils good relationships.

– Daśa. Sū. 8.38

Anger is Blind

8. A person blinded by anger destroys truth, noble conduct and humility.

– Praśna. Sū. 2.2

Forgiveness

9. By conquering anger, the soul attains forgiveness.

– Uttarā. Sū. 29.67

Consequences of Anger

10. Anger destroys the self and the rest; it destroys wealth, pleasures and righteousness; it arouses acute hatred and enmity; and drags the soul to lower existences.

– Ṛṣi. 36.13.

Inflicted by Passions

11. One who is short-tempered, ignorant, proud, harsh, hypocritical and deceitful drifts forever in the worldly current as a piece of log flowing in water.

– Daśa. Sū. 9.2.3

14. Pride

Pride

1. Ignorant is he who humiliates others out of pride.

– Sū.Kṛ.Sū. 1.13.14

Unbending Like a Pillar

2. Pride, which is unbending like a pillar of stone, drags the soul to hellish existence.

– Sthā. Sū. 4.2

Humility Brings Success

3. A person who is not proud is dear to all. Such a person alone acquires knowledge, fame and fortune and meets with success at every step.

– Bha. Ārā.1379

15. Attachment and Delusion

Shed All Attachments

1. Shed all attachments as a snake sheds its skin.

– Uttarā. Sū. 19.86

Conquering Delusion

2. The tree whose roots are arid will never flower, however much it is watered; so also if delusion is conquered, the fruit of karmas will never surface.

– Daśaśru. Sū. 5.14

Fire of Delusion

3. A little water will surface to extinguish physical fire but the waters of all the oceans will not be enough to extinguish the fire of desires and delusion.

– Ṛṣi. 3.10

Destroying Karmas

4. Once the army chief is killed, the entire army is vanquished. So also once the delusion-producing karmas are annihilated, all other karmas are destroyed.

– Daśaśru. Sū. 5.12

Suffering Due to Delusion

5. A person under delusion suffers in the cycle of birth and death.

– Ācā. Sū. 5.3

Knot of Illusion

6. Everyone knows and thinks about the acute pains of birth, old-age and death; still none develops detachment from sensual pleasures. Oh! How severe is the knot of illusion.

– Upadeśa, 204

Deceit

7. He who walks about unclad and grows lean, he who eats only once after months of rigorous fasting, if filled with deceit, will be born endless number of times.

– Sū.Kṛ.Sū. 1.2.1.9

Illusion

8. Illusion alone is enough to exterminate thousands of truths.

– Bha. Ārā.1.3.8.4

Dragged to Hell

9. Illusion, strong like the knots in a bamboo tree, drags the soul to hell.

– Sthā. Sū. 4.2

16. Desire

Greed

1. The more you get, the more you want; desire increases with every gain. What starts as a need for two grams of gold (for Kapila) grows into a desire for the entire treasure.

– Uttarā. Sū. 8.17

Increase of Greed

2. Greed increases on account of deceit and falsehood.

– Uttarā.Sū. 32. 30

Desire and Delusion

3. Just as a crane is produced from an egg and an egg from a crane, delusion springs from desire and desire from delusion.

– Uttarā. Sū. 32. 6

Boundless Avarice

4. If there were numberless mountains of gold and silver as huge as Mount Kailash, they would not satisfy an avaricious man; for avarice is boundless like the sky.

– Uttarā. Sū. 9. 48

Endless Desires

5. This entire earth with its crops of rice and barley, with its gold and cattle, all put together will not satisfy a greedy man. Knowing this, one should practise austerities.

– Uttarā. Sū. 9. 49

Influence of Greed

6. Influenced by greed, a person resorts to untruth.

– Ācā. Sū. 2.15.53

The Path to Hell

7. When greed is not controlled, it sticks to the soul like a permanent stain on cloth and drags the soul to hell.

– Shtā. Sū. 4.2

Be Not Perturbed

8. Do not be perturbed if you are unable to get expected gains.

– Daśa. Sū. 8.29

Contentment

9. By conquering greed, contentment is achieved.

– Uttarā. Sū. 29.70

Greed and Discontent

10. Can he who is always greedy, discontented, restless and mentally anguished obtain happiness?

– Bha. Ārā.1145

17. Wrong Faith

Wrong Faith

1. Owing to wrong faith, one becomes perverted. Religion is as unattractive to him as sweet juice to a person suffering from fever for he cannot relish it.

– Pañcā.1.6

Worldly Soul

2. A person with wrong faith and under the influence of strong passions considers the body and the soul to be

one. Such a soul is defined as Bahirātmā, meaning a worldly soul.

– Kārti. 193

Friend of None

3. A hostile person is friend of none and, therefore, invites enmity. This endless chain brings in its wake ceaseless misery.

– Sū.Kṛ.Sū. 1.8.7

Pride Leads to Hell

4. Pride, which is unbending like a pillar of stone, prevents a person from being humble and drags the soul to hell.

– Shtā. Sū. 4.2

Four Blemishes

5. Anger, prejudice, ingratitude and wrong faith are the four blemishes that destroy all the virtues present in a person.

– Shtā. Sū. 4.4.629

Drifting in Worldly Sojourn

6. One who is short-tempered, ignorant, proud, harsh, hypocritical and deceitful drifts in the worldly current as a piece of log drifting in a stream.

– Daśa. Sū. 9.2.3

18. Possessiveness

Attachment

1. It is on account of attachment that a person commits violence, utters lies, commits theft, indulges in sex, and develops a yearning for unlimited hoardings.

– Bhā. Pā. 132

Types of Possessiveness

2. Possessiveness is of two kinds, viz. internal and external. Internal possessions are of fourteen kinds, viz., 1. Wrong faith, 2. Carnal desire for woman, 3. Carnal desire for man, 4. Carnal desire for both, 5.

Derisive laughter, 6. Craving for pleasures, 7. Dislike for self-restraint, 8. Grief, 9. Fear, 10. Aversion, 11. Anger, 12. Pride, 13. Deceit and, 14. Greed. External possessions are of ten kinds, viz., 1. Land and farms, 2. Estates and houses, 3. Wealth and granary, 4. Clothes, 5. Utensils, 6. Servants, 7. Animals, 8. Vehicles, 9. Beds & cots, and 10. Furniture.

– Bha. Ārā.1118, 1119

Renunciation of Attachment

3. Renunciation of attachment is useful for controlling the sense organs as the mahout's hook is useful for controlling an elephant and the moat for protecting a town. Certainly, for the conquest of the senses, freedom from all possessions is a must.

– Bha. Ārā.1169

What is Attachment?

4. Attachment is possessiveness.

– Daśa. Sū. 6.21

Consequences of Evil Deeds

5. When adverse situations arise, others take away the accumulated wealth, whilst the doer must suffer the consequences of his evil deeds.

– Sū.Kṛ.Sū. 1.9.4

Causing More Enmity

6. Persons deeply engrossed in amassing wealth cause more and more enmity.

– Sū.Kṛ.Sū. 1.9.3

Knotted with Possessiveness

7. The external renunciation of a person is of no avail if his inner self is knotted with possessiveness.

– Bhā. Pā. 13

19. Attachment and Aversion

Attachment and Aversion

1. Attachment and aversion are the root causes of

karma, and karma originates from delusion. Karma is the root cause of birth and death, which is the source of misery.

– Uttarā. Sū. 32.7

Resisting Attachments

2. Attachment and aversion are two evils that lead the soul to commit sinful acts. The ascetic who always resists them does not suffer from worldly sojourn.

– Uttarā. Sū. 31.3

Uncontrolled Attachment

3. Even the most offended and powerful enemy does not cause as much harm as uncontrolled attachment and aversion do.

– Ma. Sa. 198

Boat of Austerity

4. If you desire to cross the terrible ocean of worldly existence, O virtuous one, better you quickly board the boat of austerity and self-restraint.

– Ma. Sa. 202

Block Karmic Influx

5. To attain liberation, one must block all passages of karmic influx through the three modes of activity (i.e., mind, speech and body) and conquer the sense organs and passions. One should neither commit sin, nor cause it to be done, nor approve of the sinful activities of others.

– Ma. Sa. 619

Practise Self-Control

6. One should desist from one thing and practice the other; one should give up sinful activities and practice self-control.

– Uttarā. Sū. 31.2

Resist Attachment

7. Just as a little sourness curdles milk, so also

attachment and aversion destroy the continence of an ascetic.

– Ṛṣi. 3.7

Karmic Bondage

8. Karmic bondage is low, medium or intense in direct proportion to the degree of attachment.

– Bṛ. Bhā. 2515

20. Four Deadly Passions

Four Powerful Enemies

1. Anger, pride, deceit and greed are the four powerful enemies that stimulate sinful deeds. One who desires the welfare of his self should renounce these four flaws.

– Daśa. Sū. 8.37

Conquer Your Passions

2. Conquer anger by forgiveness, pride by humility, deceit by straightforwardness and greed by contentment.

– Daśa. Sū. 8.39

Control Sense Organs

3. An aspirant should keep his mind, five sense organs, hands and feet under his control and save himself from falling prey to evil thoughts and the use of evil language.

– Sū.Kṛ.Sū. 1.8.17

Desist from Sinning

4. When a sin is committed knowingly or unknowingly, one must immediately detach oneself from the act, do penance to purify the soul and resolve not to repeat it.

– Daśa. Sū. 8.31

Fire of Passions

5. I experience peace when the fire of the four deadly passions is extinguished by the water of scriptural knowledge, noble conduct and austerity.

– Uttarā. Sū. 23.53

Insanity

6. Truly speaking, a person becomes more insane because of passions than biological imbalances.

   – Bha. Ārā.1331

Destruction of Passions

7. He who has got rid of delusions destroys his misery; he who has got rid of desire destroys his delusion; he who has got rid of greed destroys his desire; and he who owns nothing destroys his greed.

   – Uttarā. Sū. 32.8

Consequences of Passions

8. Among the four passions, anger spoils good relations, pride destroys humility, deceit destroys amity and greed destroys everything.

   – Daśa. Sū. 8.38

Contemplation of Self

9. By conquering the four passions – anger, pride, deceit and greed – and subduing the senses, be absorbed in the contemplation of the self.

   – Uttarā. Sū. 22.47

Nothing is Insignificant

10. One should not be complacent about a small debt, a slight wound, a spark of fire and any insignificant passion, because what is insignificant now may soon become uncontrollable.

    – Āva. Ni. 120

Passions and Karma

11. Karma is the root cause of worldly sojourn and passions are the cause of karma.

    – Ācā. Ni. 189

□

VI
Precepts on Conquest of Mind

21. Mind

The Bridle of Knowledge

1. I control the galloping horse by the bridle of knowledge; being controlled, it does not go astray and moves on the right path.

   – Uttarā. Sū. 23.56

Dreadful Horse

2. The mind is that fierce, unruly and dreadful horse which runs hither and thither in all directions. I control it by the discipline of dharma so that it becomes a well-trained kanthaka steed.

   – Uttarā. Sū. 23.58

Sieve-like Mind

3. The mind of man is fickle. He wants to fulfil all his desires, which is as impossible as filling a sieve with water.

   – Ācā. Sū. 1.3.2.7

Thorns of Perversion

4. Difficult it is to remove the acute thorns of perversion from the mind.

   – Sū.Kṛ. Sū. 1.2.2.11

Welcome Auspicious Thoughts

5. Relinquish all inauspicious thoughts from the

mind and let auspicious thoughts flow in from all directions.

– *Vya. Bhā. 77*

Unstill Mind

6. Just as a monkey cannot remain still even for a single moment, so also the mind cannot remain free from evil thoughts even for a single moment.

– *Bhā. Pā. 84*

Difficult to Apprehend

7. As the mind of man is unfathomable, it is difficult to apprehend it.

– *Ṛṣi. 4.6*

Reflection of the Soul

8. When the mind becomes stable like the water of a clear pond, the soul's reflection can be seen in it.

– *Tā. Sā. 41*

Genuine Ascetic

9. An ascetic (nirgrantha) is the one who has complete mastery over his mind.

– *Ācā. Sū. 2.3.15.1*

Control of Mind

10. The frenzied elephant is controlled and held captive by the chains, so also the unstable mind is controlled and held captive by the chains of knowledge.

– *Bha. Ārā. 763*

Destroy Attachment

11. Only when the mind is under control can attachment and aversion, which are the causes of worldly sufferings, be destroyed.

– *Bha. Ārā. 138*

□

VII
Precepts on Karma

22. Doctrine of Karma

Fruits of Karmas

1. Influenced by their karmas, all beings wander in the wheel of saṁsāra and suffer according to their previously acquired karmas. Without experiencing the fruit of the acquired karmas, they will never be liberated.

   – Sū.Kṛ. Sū. 1.2.1.4

Four-fold Existence

2. All living beings owe their present form of existence to their own karmas. Unable to express the endless sufferings that they undergo, they take various forms in the four-fold existence and remain fearful of birth, old age and death.

   – Sū.Kṛ. Sū. 1.2.3.18

Types of Karmas

3. The karmas, bound by which the soul wanders in the cycle of birth and death, are eight in number. They are as follows: (i) knowledge-obscuring (jñānāvarañīya), (ii) vision-obscuring (darśanavaraiṇiya). (iii) feeling-producing (vedanīya), (iv) deluding (mohanīya), (v) longevity-determining (Āyu), (vi) form-determining (Nāma),

(vii) status-determining (gotra) and (viii) power-obscuring (antarāya).

– Uttarā. Sū. 33.1, 2, 3

Mental State

4. Whenever a soul experiences a certain mental state, at that very time, it gets bound by the corresponding auspicious or inauspicious karma.

– Upadeśa, 24

When Karma Ripens

5. Just as a person is free while climbing a tree but becomes powerless when he starts falling (due to carelessness), so also the soul is free while accumulating the karma, but is helpless when karma ripens.

– Bṛ. Bhā. 2989

Who is in Control

6. At times (i.e., at the time of fruition), the living beings are controlled by karmas while at other times (i.e., at the time of action), the karmas are controlled by the living beings. Just as sometimes (while lending the money) the creditor is in a stronger position, but at the time of returning it, the debtor is in a stronger position.

– Bṛ. Bhā. 2690

Accumulation of Karmic Dirt

7. Whoever is careless about his physical activities, speech and covets wealth and women, accumulates karmic dirt of attachment and aversion in two ways just as an earthworm collects mud by both ways (by its body and mouth).

– Uttarā. Sū. 5.10

Unshared Burden

8. Neither one's kith and kin, nor one's friends and relatives can share the burden of one's sorrow. One has to bear

the sufferings all alone, because the karmas pursue the doer only.

– *Uttarā. Sū. 13.23*

Vitiate

9. Let not your mind be vitiated.

– *Sū.Kṛ. Cū. 1.2.2*

Detachment

10. Attachment binds the soul; detachment frees the soul.

– *Sa. Sā. 150*

Past Karmas

11. Past karmas will catch you definitely in the future.

– *Sū.Kṛ. Sū. 1.5.2.33*

Purification of Mind

12. As long as there is no renunciation, the ascetic cannot attain purification of mind. How can he annihilate the karma when he is of impure mind?

– *Pra. Sā. 3.20*

Accumulated Karmas

13. Just as fire quickly destroys an old, dry and hollow log of wood, so also an aspirant practising right conduct quickly destroys the accumulated karmas.

– *Āca. Ni. 234*

Bondage

14. Bondage is not due to materials but it is due to attachment and aversion.

– *Sa. Sā. 265*

Karmic Results

15. Auspicious karmas bring beneficial results and inauspicious karmas bring harmful results.

– *Aupa. Sū. 71*

No More Sprouting

16. Once the seed is burnt, it does not sprout again. So also once the karmas are destroyed, the sprouting (of these

karmic seeds) in the form of birth and death will never take place.

– Daśāśru. Sū. 5.7.15

Nirjarā

17. Those thoughts which purify the mind result in nirjarā (annihilation of karmas).

– Vya. Bhā. 6.190

Degree of Attachment

18. Karmic bondage will be less, medium or intense according to the degree of attachment in a person.

– Bṛ. Bhā. 2515

Path of Emancipation

19. Any spiritual practice by which the attachment is reduced and the accumulated karmas are annihilated is the path of emancipation as only that method of treatment is useful for curing the patient.

– Bṛ. Bhā. 3331

No Escape from Karmas

20. None can escape the effect of their own past karmas.

– Uttarā. Sū. 4.3

□

VIII
Precepts on Reflections

23. Reflections

Righteous Meditation

1. An ascetic desirous of emancipation should first practise righteous meditation (dharma dhyāna), and thereafter continue to contemplate upon the twelve-fold reflections, such as the impermanence of life, helplessness of relationships, aloneness and others as laid down.

– Dhyāna. 65

Twelve-fold Reflections

2. The twelve-fold reflections to be contemplated upon are: (i) The ephemeral nature of all things, (ii) The utter helplessness of beings in the face of death, (iii) The loneliness of each individual in the transmigratory cycle, (iv) The nature of self as distinct from body, (v) The cycle of birth and death, (vi) The nature of the constituents of the universe, (vii) Impurity of the body, (viii) Inflow of karma, (ix) Stoppage of karma, (x) Dissociation of karma, (xi) The exposition of dharma, and (xii) Rarity of enlightenment.

– Bha. Āra. 1715

Crossing the Ocean

3. An aspirant who has purified his soul by meditating on

these reflections is compared to a sailing ship. Just as a ship crosses the ocean, so also the aspirant crosses the ocean of birth and death and is released from all miseries.

– Sū.Kṛ. Sū. 1.15.5

Sublime Thoughts

4. A person who is devoid of sublime thoughts can never accomplish perfection.

– Bhā. Pā. 4

Bondage and Liberation

5. The Jaina faith stipulates that bondage and liberation depend on the thought process of each individual.

– Bhā. Pā. 116

Axe of Meditation

6. The ascetics, being noble in thought and spirit, cut the tree of transmigration with the axe of meditation.

– Bhā. Pā. 122

Noble Thoughts

7. All the thoughts expounded by the liberated ones are true. A person whose self is filled with noble thoughts always speaks the truth and is friendly towards all creatures.

– Sū.Kṛ. Sū. 1.15.3

24. Reflections on Impermanence

Pleasure is Transient

1. Time is fleeting and the nights are ticking by. The worldly pleasures are transient. Just as the birds abandon the tree when it becomes barren, so also the worldly passions desert a person who becomes impotent with time.

– Uttarā. Sū. 13.31

Impermanence of Life

2. Just as a quail pounces upon the partridge and makes it bereft of life, so also when the life-span of a person

comes to an end, death snatches him from life. Young and old, even the child in the womb, are not spared by death.

– Sū.Kṛ. Sū. 1.2.12

Lower Existence

3. Even in the absence of involvement, mere desire for sensual pleasures binds one to a lower existence.

– Uttarā. Sū. 9.53

Do Not Indulge

4. Life is inexorably advancing towards death. Old age is constantly depriving man of youthfulness and charm. O king of Pāñcāla! Listen to me, do not indulge in cardinal sins.

– Uttarā. Su. 13.26

Ephemeral

5. All the senses, beauty, health, youth, vigour, magnificence, fortune and elegance are not eternal but illusory and ephemeral like a rainbow.

– Ku. A. 4

Nothing is Permanent

6. It is natural law that whatever originates has to face extinction definitely. From this point of continued mutation, nothing is permanent and everlasting.

– Dvā. A. 4

Power of Delusion

7. It is surprising that although man sees wealth, youth and life to be transient and perishable like water bubbles, he views them as everlasting. Such is the forceful power of delusion.

– Dvā. A. 21

Transient

8. Transient like a stroke of lightning are life and beauty which you love so much. O king, why don't you contemplate on what will benefit you in life hereafter?

– Uttarā. Sū. 18.13

25. Reflections on Helplessness

No Escape

1. At the cessation of life, death grabs one's life, as the lion at one scoop takes away a deer. Mother or father or relatives - none can come to one's rescue at his crucial hour.

– Uttarā. Sū. 13.22

No Shelter

2. He is unwise who deems wealth, possessions and relatives to be his protectors and believes that they belong to him and he belongs to them. In adversity, neither can they protect nor offer him shelter.

– Sū.Kṛ. Sū. 1.2.3.16

No Protection

3. When a person is in distress, he alone bears that affliction. When his life-span comes to an end, he must depart and return alone. The wise believe that there is nothing to protect him.

– Sū.Kṛ. Sū. 1.2.3.17

No Satisfaction

4. If the entire universe belongs to you and all its treasures are yours, they still can neither satisfy your craving nor do they have the capacity to give you shelter.

– Uttarā. Sū. 14.39

No Saviour

5. A wise person should reflect thus, "Mother, father, daughter-in-law, brother, wife, sons and relatives - none can rescue from the afflictions caused by my own karmic deeds."

– Uttarā. Sū. 6.3

Birth and Death

6. In this entire world, there is not a single space-point where this soul has not experienced birth and death.

– Bha. Sū. 12.7

Renunciation

7. Renouncing his wealth, sons, relatives and possessions, leaving sorrow that never ceases, the wise should wander about without any worldly interests.

– *Sū.Kṛ. Sū. 1.9.7*

26. Reflections on the Cycle of Birth and Death

No True Happiness

1. Ever after thorough experimentation, one cannot find any essence in a plantain tree. So also one can never find true happiness from sensory pursuits.

– *Bhā. Pā. 144*

Pleasures Cause Misery

2. Sensuous enjoyments yield momentary pleasure but cause prolonged misery. By their very nature, they give maximum sorrow and minimum happiness. They are an obstacle to emancipation and a veritable mine of misfortunes.

– *Uttarā. Sū. 14.13*

Infatuated Person

3. A person suffering from itches finds pleasure in scratching his body, resulting in immense pain later on. Similarly, an infatuated person erroneously considers the sensuous enjoyment as a source of happiness.

– *Upadeśa. 212*

Knot of Delusion

4. The embodied soul knows about and reflects upon the afflictions caused by birth, old-age and death, but is unable to refrain from sensual pleasures that cause suffering. Oh! Such is the power of the knot of delusion.

– *Upadeśa. 204*

Infinite Agony

5. The soul has experienced intense physical and mental agonies infinite times and has suffered much anguish and fears.

– *Uttarā. Sū. 19/46*

Sufferings in Worldly Existence

6. Birth is misery, old age is misery and so are disease and death. All the living beings pass through nothing but suffering in this worldly existence.

– Uttarā. Sū. 19/16

Sensual Pleasures

7. O noble one, refrain from all sinful deeds. Human life is transient and will soon come to an end (make the most of life's gains). Those who are engrossed in lust and sensual pleasures will, for want of control, be deluded.

– Sū.Kṛ. Sū. 1.2.1.10

How to Escape Misery?

8. By which acts can I escape from taking birth in undesirable existences in this unstable and changing world so full of misery?

– Uttarā. Sū. 8.1

Island of Dharma

9. For living beings floating in the currents of old age and death, dharma is the one and only island, the bedrock, the refuge and the most excellent shelter.

– Uttarā. Sū.23.68

Sensual Pleasure

10. Pleasure derived through sense-organs is dependent on external factors, prone to disturbances, terminable, a cause of bondage and conflicts, and is not a source of happiness but misery only.

– Pra. Sā. 1.76

Fountain of Joy

11. What light can a lamp give to a person whose vision itself is capable of destroying darkness? In the same way, when the soul is a fountain of happiness and bliss, what joy can sensual pleasure give it?

– Pra. Sā. 1.67

27. Reflections on Solitariness

Alone at Birth and Death

1. None can share another person's sorrows. Every being is born alone and dies alone.

– Sū.Kṛ. Sū. 2.1.13

Alone While Suffering

2. Man has to bear his sorrow all alone. Neither his friends nor sons nor his relatives can share his sufferings because karma follows only the doer.

– Uttarā. Sū. 13.23

I am Alone

3. I am one and alone. Nobody is mine, nor do I belong to anybody.

– Ācā. Sū. 1.8.6

Practice Right Conduct

4. Just as the wild animal roams about all alone in a forest, so shall I practise right conduct by observing austerities and self-control on my own.

– Uttarā. Sū. 19.77

Noble or Ignoble Birth

5. Leaving behind bipeds, quadrupeds, farms, houses, wealth, food grains and everything against his will and accompanied only by his karmic deeds, the soul enters a new existence, either a noble or ignoble one.

– Uttarā. Sū. 13.24

Commits Sins

6. For the sake of his relatives and his material body, a person commits sins in this world; but at the time of reckoning, he has to bear the consequences of these sins in hell all alone.

– Bha. Ārā. 1747

28. Reflections on the Otherness of the Body

Pleasures Different from Me

1. Sensual pleasures are different and I am different.

Why then should I be attracted to things that are different?

– Sū.Kṛ. Sū. 2.1.50

Annihilate Karmas

2. The monk should annihilate the karmic body by contemplating upon the self as different from the mundane body.

– Ācā. Sū. 1.4.3

Unable to Guard

3. Sensual pleasures are unable to guard and give shelter to man and protect him. At times, man abandons the sensual pleasures and departs, and at other times, the material pleasures desert man and leave him in the lurch.

– Sū.Kṛ. Sū. 2.1.13

Lonely Death

4. Wives and sons, friends and relatives live with a person as long as he is alive. None accompanies him after death.

– Uttarā. Sū. 18.14

Practise Austerities

5. When a person dies, his body is taken to the cremation ground by his sorrowful sons and so will the parents do when their sons die. O king, understand this and practise austerities.

– Uttarā. Sū. 18.15

29. Reflections on the Impurity of the Body

Impure Body

1. This body is ephemeral, impure and of impure origin. Being subject to all kinds of sorrows and sufferings, it cannot be the eternal abode of the soul.

– Uttarā. Sū. 19.13

Abode of Illness

2. And this vain human body, an abode of illnesses and

diseases, to be swallowed up by old age and death, does not please me even for a moment.

– Uttarā. Sū. 19.15

Fountain of Bliss

3. Reflect upon the soul as distinct from this perishable body, devoid of karmas and a fountain of infinite bliss. The soul is supreme.

– Ku. A. 46

Transitory Body

4. I feel no pleasure in this transitory body which I must leave sooner or later and which is like foam or a bubble.

– Uttarā. Sū. 19.14

30. Reflections on the Inflow of Karma

Inflow of Karmas

1. There is a continuous inflow of karma through the doors of influx, such as violence etc., which enmesh the soul and engulf it in the ocean of birth and death; just as a boat with holes sinks in the sea due to the inflow of water.

– Raja.1.4.9.16

Leaky Boat

2. An ignorant aspirant is like a person being born blind getting into a leaky boat, only to be drowned before reaching the shore.

– Sū.Kṛ. Sū. 1.1.2.31

Sensuous Pleasure

3. Sensual pleasures yield momentary joy but cause prolonged misery.

– Uttarā. Sū. 14.13

Prey to Vices

4. An aspirant who has fallen prey to sensual enjoyments and vices is like a traveller who is

unable to control his horse and fails to reach his desired destination.

– *Daśa. Ni. 298*

Wandering Endlessly

5. Due to the influx of karmas, the living beings wander endlessly in the fathomless ocean of birth and death full of waves of blemishes and creatures of misery.

– *Ku. A. 56*

Self-Restraint

6. The ignorant cannot destroy the karmas but the wise annihilates them completely by self-restraint.

– *Sū.Kṛ. Sū. 1.12.15*

Karmic Inflow

7. The inflow of karmas happens through false faith, by not following the vows, due to passions and through the three channels of mind, body and speech (yoga).

– *Jaidhavalā 1.9.54*

Auspicious Influx

8. There is influx of auspicious karmas for a person who is compassionate to all living beings, whose mind is free of blemishes and whose love embraces the whole universe.

– *Pañcā.135*

31. Reflections on the Stoppage of Karma

Stopping the Influx

1. The wise knows the viciousness of the world and destroys the evils. When he stops the influx of the karmas, the previously accumulated ones too are drained.

– *Sū.Kṛ. Sū. 1.15.6*

Karmic, Bondage

2. When thousands of holes in the ship are plugged, there is no inflow of water in it. Similarly when

false faith is given up, the influx of karmic bondage is arrested.

– Naya. 155

Being Free

3. A detached monk is free from all attachments, even of his own body.

– Daśa. Sū. 6.22

Avoiding Misconduct

4. A spiritual aspirant should keep away from all those associations that generate misconduct.

– Daśa. Sū. 6.59

Merit and Demerit

5. An auspicious thought process of the soul secures merit while an inauspicious thought process causes demerit.

– Pañcā.132

Restricting the Influx

6. The influx of karmas caused by false faith, not practising the vows, passions and yoga is restricted by having right faith, taking the vows, practising forgiveness and by controlling the body, mind and speech.

– Mū. 241

Indifferent to Senses

7. A person who is indifferent to sensual pleasures traverses the forest of birth and death.

– Jñātā. 1.6

Self-Control

8. Self-control of only such a person is praiseworthy who has neither attachment nor aversion of any kind, be it of sound, form, smell, taste or touch.

– Daśa. Ni. 295

Prevention of Desires

9. An aspirant, by practising self-denial, shuts as it were, all the doors of the āsrava; prevents desires from rising in

him and thus becomes indifferent and serene towards all subjects.

– Uttarā. Sū. 29.14

Stopping Inflow of Karmas

10. A person having renounced all sensual pleasures and keeping himself away from all alluring things so long dear to him stops the inflow of karmas.

– Dvā. A. 101

Emancipation

11. Emancipation results from cessation of the influx of karmic bondage. Hence, a noble soul desirous of stopping the influx should contemplate upon stopping it.

– Mū. 743

32. Reflections on the Dissociation of Karmas

Dissociation of Karmas

1. Just as a coated wall becomes thin when the coat is removed, so also the karmic body is emaciated by austerities.

– Sū.Kṛ. Sū. 1.2.1.14

Arrow of Penance

2. When the arrow of penance pierces the armour of karma, the monk wins the battle of transmigration and is released from the cycle of birth and death.

– Uttarā. Sū. 9.22

Restrain Yourself

3. Restrain yourself and annihilate all karmas.

– Ācā. Sū.1.4.3.32

Annihilation of Karmas

4. For an endeavouring aspirant, the karmic bondage becomes less and less as the karmas are subsequently annihilated. Consequently, he is very soon emancipated.

– Ni. Bhā. 3335

Blocking the Inlets

5. The water of a huge pond is gradually drained when its inlets of water supply are blocked and the previously accumulated water is either drained out or evaporates. Similarly, the karmas of an ascetic that have accumulated in innumerable births are annihilated by blocking the entrance of sinful deeds through austerities.

– *Uttarā. Sū. 30.5,6*

Unmoved by the Winds

6. Just as a mountain remains unmoved by gusty winds, so also a person absorbed in the self remains unmoved by pleasant or unpleasant and favourable or unfavourable circumstances.

– *Sū.Kṛ. Sū. 1.1.37*

Forsaking Pleasures

7. There is intense destruction of karmas when a person capable of enjoying the sensual pleasures forsakes them. He certainly attains the greatest benefit of emancipation.

– *Bha. Sū. 7.7*

33. Reflections on Rarity of Enlightenment

1. Why don't you understand that it is rare to obtain right understanding afterwards (after death). The nights that once pass do not return. Similarly, it is not easy to obtain human birth once again.

– *Sū.Kṛ. Sū. 1.2.1.1*

Practise Dharma

2. Dharma can be practised only in human form (hence, human life should be utilised properly).

– *Sū.Kṛ. Sū. 1.15.15*

Rarity of Human Birth

3. Wake up, man! Birth in lower existences is full of fear. Hence, understand the rarity of human

birth and seek self-realisation. The universe is full of sorrow and sufferings like a man who has caught fever. An ignorant person seeking happiness from his deeds (violence, etc.) meets only with misery.

– Sū.Kṛ. Sū. 1.7.11

Proper Utilisation of Birth

4. A person who does not utilise his human birth well cannot acquire it once again. Without the human form, enlightenment is difficult. He cannot get again such mental disposition appropriate for practising right conduct.

– Sū.Kṛ. Sū. 1.15.18

34. Reflections on Dharma

Fruitless Nights

1. The days and nights that pass will never return. They bear no fruit for him who does not abide by Dharma.

– Uttarā. Sū. 14.24

Fruitful Nights

2. The days and nights that pass will never return. They bear fruit only for him who does abide by dharma.

– Uttarā. Sū. 14.25

Practise Dharma

3. One should practise dharma before old age creeps up, the senses become feeble and he falls a prey to all kinds of diseases.

– Daśa. Sū. 8.36

Give up Vicious Acts

4. A person who is attached to his parents and others cannot acquire a noble birth in his next life. Knowing these causes of dangers, one should take vows and give up all vicious acts, which lead to violence.

– Sū.Kṛ. Sū. 1.2.1.3

Annihilate Karmas

5. Just as a bird flutters its wings and removes the dust by shaking itself, so the spiritual aspirant engrossed in austerities, annihilates the accumulated karmas of previous births.

   – *Sū.Kṛ. Sū. 1.2.1.15*

Rarity

6. Easily obtainable are the enchanting pleasures of the world and the affluence of the gods; easy also it is to get sons and friends; but difficult it is to follow dharma.

   – *Prāstāvika*

Uncertain Tomorrow

7. He who can call death his friend, who can escape from its clutches, and who is sure never to die – only he can postpone his duties till tomorrow.

   – *Uttarā. Sū. 14.27*

Why be Indolent?

8. "I have this and I have not that, this I must do and this I should not do." Even while a man nurtures such thoughts, death lays its jaws on him. Why then should a person be indolent?

   – *Uttarā. Sū. 14.15*

□

IX

Precepts on Righteousness (Dharma)

35. Righteousness

Celestials Revere

1. Dharma is supremely auspicious. Its constituents are non-violence, self-restraint and austerity. Even the celestials revere him who is rooted in righteousness.

– Daśa. Sū.1.1

What is Dharma?

2. The essential nature of any substance is dharma. The ten virtues such as forgiveness constitute dharma. The triple jewels, i.e., right faith, right knowledge and right conduct, comprise dharma. Giving protection to living creatures is also dharma.

– Dvā. A. 478

Ten Characteristics of Dharma

3. Supreme forgiveness, supreme humility, supreme straightforwardness, supreme truthfulness, supreme purity, supreme self-restraint, supreme austerity, supreme renunciation, supreme detachment and supreme continence are the ten characteristics of dharma.

– Ku. A. 70

True Renunciation

4. He alone can be said to have truly renounced (the world) who has turned his back on all available,

desirable, beloved and dear objects which are entirely his own.

– Daśa. Sū.2.3

Superiority of Restraint

5. Greater is he who restrains himself, though giving no alms, than he who gives thousands and thousands of cows every month but restrains not himself.

– Uttarā. Sū. 9.40

Noble Householder

6. Noble is that householder who earns his livelihood by fair means.

– Sū.Kṛ. Sū.2.2.39

Wisdom

7. The highest wisdom makes it possible for one to recognise dharma and ascertain the reality of things.

– Uttarā. Sū. 23.25

Shelter to Homeless

8. One should always be prepared to give shelter to the homeless and help to the helpless.

– Sthā. Sū. 8

Ideal Wife

9. An ideal wife is one who helps the cause of dharma, is absorbed in dharma, and shares her husband's pleasure and pain equally.

– Upā. Sū. 7.22.7

Householders and Monks

10. Some householders are superior to certain monks in self-control, but the ascetics practising right conduct are superior to all householders who practise self-restrain.

– Utt.Sū.5.20

The Pure

11. He who is simple is pure, and dharma abides with him who is pure.

– Uttarā. Sū. 3.12

Prosper Always

12. May you prosper with the aid of knowledge, faith, conduct, forbearance and perfection.

– Uttarā. Sū. 22.26

Human Birth is Capital

13. Human birth is capital, proper utilisation of this capital begets heavenly world; improper utilisation engenders sub-human existences.

– Uttarā. Sū. 7.16

Compassion

14. Purity in compassion is dharma.

– Bo. Pā. 25

The Ideal Monk

15. Even the celestials desire to meet that monk who follows a diet regimen and has conquered his senses.

– Daśaśru. Sū. 5.4

Gateways of Dharma

16. Forgiveness, contentment, simplicity and modesty – these form the four gateways of righteousness (dharma).

– Sthā. Sū.4.4

36. Code of Conduct for Monks

Kinds of Dharma

1. The Śramaṇa dharma is of ten kinds, viz., forgiveness, freedom from greed, simplicity, modesty, humility, truthfulness, self-restraint, austerity, renunciation and celibacy.

– Sthā. Sū. 10

Articles of Creed

2. The eight articles of creed (Pravacana Mātā) for the monks are the vigilances (Samitis) and restraints (Guptis). There are five Samitis and three Guptis.

– Uttarā. Sū. 24.1

Vigilances and Restraints

3. The five vigilances (Samitis) are: to be vigilant while walking (Īryā samiti), conversing (Bhāṣā samiti), begging for alms (Eṣaṇā samiti), upkeep of things necessary for religious conduct (Ādāna samiti) and careful disposal of waste (Uccāra samiti). The three restraints (Guptis) are: perfect mind control (Mano-gupti), ideal restraint of speech (Vāk-gupti) and exemplary control over body (Kāya-gupti).

– Uttarā. Sū. 24.2

Moderation

4. A self-restrained aspirant eats, drinks and talks less.

– Sū.Kṛ. Sū. 1.8.25

Detached Monks

5. Just as a bee gathers honey from many flowers and satisfies itself without harming them, so also the detached monks, who are free from all possessions, get their food from different householders without being a burden on them.

– Daśaśru. Sū. 1.2.3

Cross the Worldly Ocean

6. The body is called the boat, the soul is the oarsman and the cycle of birth and death is the ocean which is crossed by the great sages.

– Uttarā. Sū. 23.73

True Monk

7. A true monk is one who has no yearnings, who is indifferent to this world, whose diets and movements are proper, and who is free from passions.

– Pra. Sā. 3.26

Ignorance

8. The monk who is lacking in scriptural knowledge neither knows his self nor the things other than his self.

– Pra. Sā. 3.33

Right View

9. Unlike other persons, the self-realised monk sees through the eyes of the agamas.

– Pra. Sā. 3.34

Awakened Soul

10. Thekarmicbondage,destroyedbyanunenlightenedsoul by practising austerities in crores of births, is achieved only in one breath by an awakened soul practising the three restraints.

– Pra. Sā. 3.38

Truly Initiated

11. He who looks at both straw and gold alike is said to be truly initiated.

– Bo. Pā. 47

Purpose of Eating

12. A great monk eats only for the sustenance of life and not for the pleasure of it.

– Uttarā. Sū. 35.17

Uncontrolled Passions

13. Even after becoming a monk, if the passions such as anger are not controlled, his monkhood is useless like the flower of sugarcane plant.

– Daśa. Ni. 301

A True Monk

14. The exaltation of forgiveness, humility, simplicity, greedlessness, modesty, forbearance and the faithful observation of the prescribed code of conduct are the hallmarks of a monk.

– Daśa. Ni. 349

Detachment

15. The practice of detachment severs the bonds of attachment and desire.

– Uttarā. Sū. 29.45

Heart of the Monk

16. The heart of a monk is as pure as the autumnal waters, as free as the birds and as enduring as the earth.

– Sū.Kṛ. Sū. 2.2.21

Restrained Monk

17. A restrained monk accepts whatever food is prepared for the householders and offered to him as if it were butter and honey, irrespective of its being hot, bitter, pungent, salty, sweet or sour.

– Daśaśru. Sū. 5.1.97

Noble Birth

18. A laity who gives alms selflessly and a detached monk both beget noble births.

– Daśaśru. Sū. 5.1.100

Observing Austerity

19. If a monk doesn't get the ideal food, he should not grieve but look upon it as an opportunity to observe austerity.

– Daśaśru. Sū. 5.2.6

Hankering after Honour

20. A monk, who hankers after honour, fame, status and respect, indulges in sinful acts, and still, in order to preserve his untarnished image, seeks to hide his acts.

– Daśaśru. Sū. 5.2.35

Enlightened Monk

21. An enlightened monk does not indulge even a little in deceit and untruth.

– Daśaśru. Sū. 5.2.49

Toleration of Suffering

22. A monk bears hunger, thirst, discomfort, cold, heat, fear and anguish with an unperturbed mind. Toleration of suffering caused to the body because of this will entail him great benefits.

– Daśa. Sū. 8.27

All Creatures Suffer

23. "It is not I alone who suffer but all creatures in the world too suffer." Thus, a wise man should ruminate and patiently bear the afflictions that befall him, without giving way to his passions.

– Sū.Kṛ. Sū. 1.2.1.13

A True Monk

24. A true monk is one whose limbs, speech and senses are under his control, who is forever immersed in the contemplation of the self, and who understands the true spirit of the scriptures.

– Daśa. Sū. 10.15

Spiritual Contemplation

25. A true monk is one who is not proud of his own lineage, beauty, gains and scriptural knowledge. Thus discarding all pride, he remains deeply immersed in spiritual contemplation.

– Daśa. Sū. 10.19

Qualities of a Monk

26. A monk should be compassionate towards all; he should be of a forbearing nature, restrained and chaste. He should renounce all sinful activities and live with his senses under control.

– Uttarā. Sū. 21.13

Blissful Emancipation

27. A monk who is totally detached, calm and serene attains that blissful emancipation which even a Chakravarti (universal monarch) cannot ever have.

– Bha. Ā. 1182

37. Who is a Śramaṇa?

Who is a Śramaṇa?

1. One does not become a monk by merely tonsuring; nor a Brāhmaṇa by reciting the Oṁkāra Mantra; nor

a muni by living in the forest; nor a hermit by wearing clothes woven out of the kuśa grass.

– *Uttarā. Sū.* 25.31

A Monk by Equanimity

2. A person becomes a monk by equanimity, a Brāhmaṇa by his celibacy, a muni by his knowledge and a hermit by his austerities.

– *Uttarā. Sū.* 25.32

Worthy of Veneration

3. A person becomes monk by his virtues and a pseudo-monk by absence of virtues; therefore, master all the virtues of a monk and be free from all the vices of one who is not a monk. A person who knows his self through the self and maintains equanimity towards attachment and aversion is worthy of veneration.

– *Daśaśru. Sū.* 9.3.11

Equanimous Aspirant

4. A true monk maintains equanimity in his success and failure, happiness and misery, life and death, blame and praise, and honour and dishonour.

– *Uttarā. Sū.* 19.91

A Brāhmaṇa by his Deeds

5. According to one's deeds, one becomes a Brāhmaṇa, a kṣatriya, a vaiśya or sudra.

– *Uttarā. Sū.* 25.33

38. Code of Conduct for Householders

Śrāvaka

1. A Śrāvaka is one who is endowed with right faith and who listens everyday to the sermons of the monks about right conduct.

– *Sāvaya.* 2

Religion of Householder

2. The five primary vows (aṇuvratas), the three meritorious

vowsm (Guṇvratas) and the four disciplinary vows (Śiksāvratas) are the twelve kinds of vows prescribed for a householder.

– Sāvaya. 6

Seven Vices

3. The seven vices (from which a householder should abstain) are: 1. Sexual contact with another woman, 2. Gambling, 3. Taking intoxicants, 4. Hunting, 5. Uttering harsh words, 6. Giving disproportionate punishment, and 7. Misappropriation of other's property.

– Bṛ. Bhā. 940

Consumption of Meat

4. Consumption of meat arouses one's passions; this leads him to take intoxicants and indulge in gambling. Thus, he falls prey to all the above vices.

– Vasu. Śrā. 88

Five Primary Vows

5. The five primary vows (aṇuvratas) are partial abstinence from violence, untruth, stealing, carnality and possessiveness.

– Ātur. Pra. 3

Merciful Attitude

6. Even if one is a householder, if he is merciful and fair to all living beings and treats everyone as equal, he can acquire a celestial birth.

– Sū.Kṛ. Sū. 1.2.3.13

Equal to a Saint

7. While observing the vow of equanimity (Sāmāyika), a householder becomes equal to a saint.

– Vi. Bhā. 2690

Not Contradictory

8. Some view righteousness, wealth and pleasure as different and contradictory. Jaina faith, however,

propounds that if these are imbibed in the true spirit, then they will only be complementary.

– *Daśa. Ni.* 262

True Śrāvaka

9. A true Śrāvaka is one who observes the vows, practises noble conduct, engages himself in scriptural and self-study, is simple and modest, serves the spiritual master and is at ease in discourses.

– *Dharma-ratna-Prakaraṇa* 33

39. Non-Violence

Non-Violence

1. Not to kill any living being is the quintessence of all wisdom. Certainly, one has to understand that non-violence and equality of all living beings are essentials of dharma.

– *Sū.Kṛ. Sū.* 1.11.10

Eternal Virtues

2. Knowledge of living and non-living alone will enable one to be compassionate towards all living creatures. Knowing this, all aspirants proceed from knowledge to eternal virtues. What can an ignorant do? How does he know what is noble and what is evil?

– *Daśa. Sū.* 4.10

Reflect on Oneness

3. O man! Think that the being whom you want to kill is none else but you; he too experiences happiness and sorrow just like you. Think about this – the being whom you wish to govern and enslave is none else but you. Also think about this – the being whom you wish to hurt and harm is none else but you, the being whom you want to punish and drive away is also none else but you.

– *Ācā. Sū.* 1.5.5.101

Practising Non-Violence

4. An ingenuous and self-disciplined person, therefore, neither harms nor kills any living being nor does he cause them to be harmed and killed by others. One has to bear the consequences of one's actions. Hence, never desire to harm any living being.

– Ācā. Sū. 1.5.5.101

Ahimsā is Highest Religion

5. Nothing is higher than Mount Meru, nor anything more expansive than the sky. Similarly, know that no dharma is equal to ahimsā in this world.

– Bha. Pa. 91

40. Truthfulness

Truthful

1. A person who speaks the truth becomes trustworthy like a mother, venerable like a preceptor and dear to everyone like a kinsman.

– Bha. Ā. 840

Truth is Wisdom

2. Truth is the quintessence of all wisdom in this world. Truth is more tranquil and deeper than the deepest ocean.

– Praśna. 2.2

Vision of Truth

3. Just as a blind man is unable to see anything despite the presence of light, so also an ignorant person cannot have a vision of the truth in spite of the presence of thescriptures.

– Sū.Kṛ. Sū. 1.12.8

Divine Truth

4. Truth is God.

– Praśna. Sū. (Saūvardvāra) 2

Transcending Death

5. A wise person who treads the path of truth transcends death.

– Ācā. Sū. 1.3.66

Falsehood

6. In this world, falsehood is condemned by all saints. A person who utters a lie is trusted by none. Hence, one should give up falsehood.

– Daśa. Sū. 6.13

Remains Unmoved

7. A person who practises truthfulness remains unmoved in the face of severe trials and tribulations.

– Ācā. Sū. 1.3.3

Door for Sins

8. Lord Jinendra has stated that falsehood is the door through which sins step in.

– Bha. Ā. 489

Source of Noble Qualities

9. Truthfulness is the abode of austerity, self-restraint and all other virtues. Indeed, truthfulness is the source of all noble qualities as the ocean is for fish.

– Bha. Ā. 842

41. Non-Stealing

Forms of Stealing

1. Covetousness, attachment, greed, non-restraint, desire, stealing, malpractices in trade and commerce and taking others' articles without their permission form part of various types of stealing.

– Praśna. 1.3.10

Creating Enmity

2. As theft is the cause of disrepute, noble people do not indulge in it. It is decried by all saints. It creates enmity amongst friends and relatives. It causes much attachment and avarice.

– Praśna. 1.3.9

Taking Without Permission

3. A mendicant should not take anything animate or inanimate, whether cheap or expensive, not even a toothpick without permission of the owner.

– Daśa. Sū. 6.14

Indulges in Theft

4. Under the influence of greed, a man fails to discriminate between good and evil and indulges in theft without caring even for his own life.

– Bha. Ā. 857

Buying Stolen Property

5. Buying stolen property, smuggling goods, disobeying the rules of law, use of false weights and measures and adulteration – all these are classified as theft.

– Sāvaya. 268

Tempted to Steal

6. Only when a person falls prey to greed is he tempted to steal another's property.

– Uttarā. Sū. 32.29

42. Celibacy

Brahmacarya

1. The soul verily is Brahma. So, the activity regarding the self of an ascetic, who refrains from seeking enjoyment through other's body (i.e., sexual enjoyment) is called Brahmacarya (celibacy).

– Bha. Ā. 878

Celibate

2. A celibate should give up the sensual pleasure of sound, sight, smell, taste and touch.

– Uttarā. Sū. 16.10

Difficult Vow

3. He observes the most difficult but pious virtue of celibacy, who is neither infatuated nor attracted even after observing feminine charms.

– Ku. A. 11.80

Loss of Character

4. Just as a jar filled with lac when subjected to fire melts quickly and is destroyed, so does a monk who indulges in sexual contact with women lose his character.

   – Sū.Kṛ. Sū. 1.4.1.27

True Renouncer

5. He who is unable to enjoy apparels, perfume, jewellery, women and cosy cushions because of their non-availability is not a true ascetic. On the other hand, a person who turns his back to all worldly pleasures easily available and dear to him is a true renouncer.

   – Daśa. Sū. 2.2.3

Attraction of Women

6. To a man who longs for liberation, who is afraid of the saṁsāra and lives according to dharma, even for him nothing in this world offers so many difficulties as the attraction of women who lure the mind of the ignorant.

   – Uttarā. Sū. 32.17

Overcoming Attachments

7. One who has overcome sensual attachments and can overcome all other temptations of his life as easily as a person who has crossed the great ocean will not face any difficulty in crossing the river like Ganges.

   – Uttarā. Sū. 32.18

Tasty Food

8. One should not relish tasty foods for they stimulate the passions. Just as birds flock towards a tree laden with fruits, so also a person is impassioned by taking tasty food.

   – Uttarā. Sū. 32.10

Excessive Food

9. Just as a forest conflagration is difficult to be extinguished in the presence of the winds, so also are the senses of a person who relishes tasty food

not easily calmed. Hence, a celibate should not eat excessive food.

– Uttarā. Sū. 32.11

Fire of Lust

10. The fire of lust, when kindled by the fuel of desires, destroys the forest of the three worlds. Blessed is he whose youth remains unsullied by this fire.

– Bha. Ā. 1115

Company of Women

11. For men observing celibacy, the company of women is not permitted; and for women observing celibacy, the company of men is condemned.

– Bha. Ā. 988

Virtuous Women

12. There are many virtuous women who are famous for their purity and chastity. They are like the goddesses on this earth and even revered by gods.

– Bha. Ā. 995

Celibacy is Greatest

13. Just as the moon is unsurpassed and outshines the planets and stars, so also is celibacy the greatest of all the qualities, viz. modesty, chastity, penance, vows and others. Verily, celibacy is God.

– Praśna. 2.4.27

Spiritual Aspirant

14. Just as the wind passes through the flames of fire, so also a spiritual aspirant overcomes the charms of beautiful women and supersedes their attractions. They are first to get liberated.

– Sū.Kṛ. Sū. 1.15.8.9

Conquer Passions

15. J ust as the river Vaitaraṇī (the river in hell) is difficult to cross, so also it is very difficult for an ignorant person to conquer over the passions for women.

– Sū.Kṛ. Sū. 1.3.4.16

Revering the Celibate

16. The devas, dānavas, gandharvas, yakṣas, rākṣasas and kinnaras pay homage to a celibate monk who stands rooted in the difficult vow of celibacy.

– *Uttarā. Sū. 16.16*

43. Non-Possession

Insatiable Desires

1. Even if this whole world full of wealth is given to a man, he will not be content, for it is very difficult to satisfy the desires of an avaricious man.

– *Uttarā. Sū. 8.16*

Wealth and Liberation

2. Wealth, movable and immovable possessions, granary and other domestic articles cannot relieve a person from bondage caused by one's own karmas.

– *Uttarā. Sū. 6.6*

Final Departure

3. One should reflect thus, "One day I have to abandon all the wealth and property, treasures and fortunes, relatives and friends and even this body and depart from this world."

– *Uttarā. Sū. 19.17*

Liberates from Karmic Bondage

4. A person who knows that wealth and relatives are incapable of protecting him and that life is ephemeral is liberated from the karmic bondage.

– *Sū.Kṛ. Sū. 1.1.5*

Reasonable Profits

5. A noble householder is one who does not buy valuable goods on much below their cost price, does not take possession of lost properties and remains satisfied by earning reasonable profits.

– *Dvā. A. 335*

Wealth Cannot Protect

6. Wealth cannot protect an imprudent person in this birth and the next. Just as an extinguished lamp cannot light the path, so also a person who is deluded cannot tread the right path.

   – Uttarā. Sū. 4.5

The Path of Hell

7. Ignorant persons who earn money through evil deeds fall into the snares of their passions and earn the resentment of others, leave all the wealth here and go to hell.

   – Uttarā. Sū. 4.2

Imprudent Person

8. An imprudent person engrossed in violence does not understand that the life is perishable, and being attached to worldly objects, dares to commit sins. He toils day and night. That rash and foolish person assumes his body to be imperishable and tries to earn more and more wealth.

   – Sū.Kṛ. Sū. 1.10.18

Establish in Dharma

9. Knowing that wealth is the cause of misery, the fetter of egoism and the source of many dangers, one should establish oneself in dharma, which is gratifying, unequalled, unsurpassed and which generates those qualities that yield the fruit of emancipation.

   – Uttarā. Sū. 9.99

44. Austerity

1. He who controls the senses and passions and concentrates on the self through meditation and scriptural study observes austerity definitely.

   – Adh. Sā. 18.156

Kinds of Austerities

2. Austerities are of two kinds: external and internal.

External austerities are of six kinds and internal austerities also are of six kinds.

– *Uttarā. Sū. 30.7*

External Austerities

3. External austerities are: 1. Fasting, 2. Eating less than one's normal diet, 3. Seeking alms, 4. Abstention from tasty food, 5. Mortification of the body, and 6. Solitude.

– *Uttarā. Sū. 30.8*

True Fasting

4. That fasting is true when the person observing it does not entertain any inauspicious thoughts, whose senses do not become weak and whose activities of mind, speech and body remain unimpaired.

– *Ma. Sa. 134*

Practise Fasting Carefully

5. A person should practise fasting only after taking into consideration his physical strength, prowess, devotion, state of health and the knowledge of time and place.

– *Daśa. Sū. 8.35*

Annihilation of Karmas

6. As a large tank whose supply of water has been blocked gradually drains by consumption and evaporation, so do the karmas of a self-restrained monk accumulated over millions of births get annihilated by austerities, if there is no fresh influx of karmas.

– *Uttarā. Sū. 30.5,6*

Internal Austerities

7. Internal austerities are (of six kinds): 1. Expiation of sins, 2. Reverence, 3. Service, 4. Scriptural study, 5. Meditation, and 6. Renunciation.

– *Uttarā. Sū. 30.30*

Higher Existence

8. Persons who tread the path of knowledge, faith, conduct and austerity get higher existence.

– *Uttarā. Sū. 28.3*

Caste Unimportant

9. The importance of austerity is obvious, but there is no evidence that caste is important.

– Uttarā. Sū. 12.37

The Great Sacrifice

10. I perform the sacrifice which has been regarded as the greatest by the sages wherein austerity is the fire, the self is the hearth, right exertion is the sacrificial ladle, karma is the fuel, and self-restraint and tranquillity are the oblations.

– Uttarā. Sū. 12.44

Destroy the Passions

11. We do not extol the emaciated body of the aspirant observing fasts. Truly speaking, one must emaciate or destroy the longings of sensual pleasures, passions and the ego.

– Ni. Bhā. 3758

Purifying the Soul

12. By observing austerity, one acquires the power to destroy the karmas and purify his soul.

– Uttarā. Sū. 29.28

Practise to Destroy Karmas

13. One should not practise austerities for this life or the hereafter. Also one should not do it for praise, status, fame or name. One should practise austerities only to destroy the karmas.

– Daśāśru. Sū. 9.4.4

45. Forgiveness

Forbearance

1. His forbearance is perfect, who does not get excited with anger even when terrible afflictions are caused to him by celestials, human beings and animals.

– Kārti. 364

Enmity towards None

2. I forgive all living beings, may all living beings forgive me. I cherish friendliness towards all and harbour enmity towards none.

– Āva. Sū. 4.5

Forgiveness

3. Renouncing all passions and delusions with a pure heart, I beg your forgiveness if I have not been prudent in my behaviour towards you inadvertently.

– Bṛ. Bhā. 1368

Spirit of Forgiveness

4. When anger is conquered, the spirit of forgiveness springs in the soul.

– Uttarā. Sū. 29.67

Infinite Happiness

5. The soul experiences infinite joy through forgiveness.

– Uttarā. Sū. 29.19

Begging Pardon

6. I beg pardon of one and all if, due to attachment and aversion, I have been ungrateful to them or if my speech has been inappropriate and objectionable.

-Mū. 58

46. Equipoise

Attachment to Hearing

1. Sound is the object of ears. Difficult it is to ignore when one hears something. A monk renounces attachment and aversion to whatever he hears.

– Āva. Cū. 2.15.72

Attachment to Seeing

2. Sight is the object of eyes. Difficult it is to ignore when one sees something. A monk renounces attachment and aversion to whatever he sees.

– Āva. Cū. 2.15.73

Attachment to Smell

3. Smell is the object of nose. Difficult it is to ignore when one smells something. A monk renounces attachment and aversion to whatever he smells.

   – *Āva. Cū. 2.15.74*

Attachment to Taste

4. Taste is the object of tongue. Difficult it is to ignore when one eats or drinks something. A monk renounces attachment and aversion to whatever he tastes.

   – *Āva. Cū. 2.15.75*

Attachment to Touch

5. Touch is the object of body. Difficult it is to ignore when one touches something. A monk renounces attachment and aversion to whatever he touches.

   – *Āva. Cū. 2.15.76*

Equanimity

6. Right conduct is really what constitutes religion, which, in turn, is pointed out as equanimity. Equanimity is that state when one contemplates on the soul and which is free from delusion and agitation.

   – *Pra. Sā. 17*

Indifferent to Joy and Sorrow

7. A monk is said to be absorbed in pure consciousness if he is indifferent to joy and sorrow.

   – *Pra. Sā. 1.14*

No Inflow of Karmas

8. There is no inflow of auspicious and inauspicious karmas for a person who has neither attachment nor aversion for any object, who is not deluded and who is indifferent to joy and sorrow.

   – *Pañcā. 142*

Noble Persons

9. Noble persons patiently bear the harsh, wounding and humiliating utterances of the wicked.

   – *Bhā. Pā. 107*

Impartiality

10. Looking at everyone with an impartial mind, one should not do anything either to favour or to harm them.

– *Sū.Kṛ. Sū. 1.10.7*

Equanimity

11. To treat as equal a piece of straw and gold, a friend and a foe, as also to develop a mind devoid of attachment and progressively inclined towards virtuous conduct, this is what constitutes sāmāyika.

– *Ni. Cū. 2846*

Sense Conquest

12. A person is said to have conquered his senses if he has neither attraction nor aversion for the sensual pleasures of sound, form, smell, taste and touch.

– *Daśa. Ni. 295*

47. Non-Attachment

No Attachment

1. A spiritual aspirant should neither cherish a desire to live nor long for death. He should remain neutral and have no attachment for life as well as death.

– *Ācā. Sū. 1.8.8.4*

Detachment

2. A person who is detached, though living in the world, is not affected by it, just as the leaf of the lotus is not moistened by water.

– *Uttarā. Sū. 32.47*

Free from Desires

3. Nothing is impossible in this world for a person who is free from all desires.

– *Uttarā. Sū. 19.45*

Untimely Ruin

4. He who is passionately fond of beauty will come to

untimely ruin; just as an impassioned moth drawn by the light rushes to its death.

– Uttarā. Sū. 32.24

Impure Mind

5. As long as there is no renunciation (absolutely) free from (any) expectation, the monk cannot have purification of mind, how can he annihilate the karmas, when he is impure in mind?

– Pra. Sā. 3.20

Cannot Renounce

6. A person who has attachments cannot renounce the world.

– Bṛ. Bhā. 3385

Give up All Expectations

7. O Serene One! Give up all expectations, desires and prodigality.

– Ācā. Sū. 1.2.4.86

Detachment

8. Just as gold fallen in the sludge remains untainted, so also a self-realised person while doing his worldly duties is not tainted by karmas. On the other hand, just as iron gets rusty when it falls in the sludge, so also an ignorant person who is full of attachment while performing his duties is bound by karmas.

– Sa. Sā. 218-219

48. Straightforwardness

Virtue of Straightforwardness

1. He who does not think crookedly does not act crookedly, does not speak crookedly and does not hide his own weaknesses, observes the virtue of straightforwardness.

– Dvā. A. 396

Filled with Deceit

2. Even if a person walks about unclad and mortifies his

flesh by observing austerities and fasts for months together, if filled with deceit, he will be born endless number of times.

– Sū.Kṛ. Sū. 1.2.1.9

Ignorant Person

3. If an ignorant person observes long fasts for several months and takes just a morsel of food to break each fast, he still will not be equal to the sixteenth part of the religious order preached by the Jainas.

– Uttarā. Sū. 9.44

Gains Humility

4. By conquering deceit, a person gains humility.

– Uttarā. Sū. 29.69

Confession

5. Just as a child speaks of his good and bad acts in an innocent manner, similarly, one ought to confess one's guilt with a mind free from deceit and pride.

– Mahā. Pra. 22

Atonement

6. A person who atones for the misdeeds he has committed carelessly is a true aspirant.

– Sthā. Sū. 8

49. Modesty

Practising Humility

1. A monk who does not flaunt even slightly his family lineage, looks, caste, learning, austerity, scriptural knowledge and character practises humility.

– Ku. A. 72

Commanding Respect

2. He truly commands respect who is always cautious not to insult others. A person who merely boasts but has no virtues cannot command respect.

– Bha. Ā. 1429

None is High nor Low

3. Every person has been born several times in high caste as well as in low caste; hence none is either high or low. Knowing this, who will experience pride about taking birth in a respectable or high caste? And who will evince attachment to any particular caste?

– *Ācā. Sū.1.2.3.49-50*

Modest

4. When pride is overcome, a person becomes modest.

– *Uttarā. Sū. 29.63*

Disliked

5. A person who is proud is disliked by all. He definitely confronts conflicts, enmity, fear, grief and disrespect in this world and the next.

– *Bha. Ā. 1377*

50. Total Detachment

I am Alone

1. I am alone, pure, eternal, formless and full of knowledge and vision. Other than this, not even an atom of any object is mine.

– *Sa. Sū. 1.38*

Sleep Happily

2. A person who is content and does not desire a share in others' profits sleeps happily.

– *Sthā. Sū. 4.3*

Non-Possessiveness

3. That mendicant alone acquires the virtue of non-possessiveness, who, having renounced the sense of ownership and attachment and controlling his thoughts, remains unperturbed by feelings of pleasure and pain.

– *Ku. A. 79*

51. Charity

Kinds of Charity

1. Charity is said to be of four kinds, viz. that of food, medicine, scriptural teaching and assurance of protection to all living beings. According to the code of conduct of householders, this four-fold charity is declared worthy of performance.

– Vasu. Śra. 233

Bliss of Emancipation

2. A householder who eats after giving alms to monks enjoys the best material comforts and will gradually obtain the bliss of emancipation. Such is the preaching of the Jainas.

– Ra. Sā. 22

Protection to All

3. Of all kinds of charity, the charity of giving protection to living beings in fear of death is known as abhayadāna, which is supreme amongst all charities.

– Vasu. Śra. 238

Important Virtue

4. Charity is the most important virtue of every member of the laity.

– Ra. Sā. 11

Selfless Donor

5. A selfless donor (alms-giver) and a detached monk who practises faultless begging are rare. Both eventually acquire noble birth.

– Daśaśru. Sū. 5.1.100

□

X
Precepts on Meditation

52. Meditation

Meditation is Fundamental

1. Just as the head is the most important of the body and the roots for the tree, meditation is fundamental to all religious practices of a monk.

– *Ṛṣi. 22.13*

Steady Mind

2. A steady state of mind constitutes meditation while an active mind might be engaged in either contemplation or deep reflection or apprehension.

– *Dhyāna. 2*

No Attachment or Aversion

3. A person who has no attachment, aversion and delusion and whose mind, speech and body are steadfast, burns all auspicious and inauspicious karmas in the fire of meditation.

– *Pañcā. 146*

Concentration of Mind

4. For monks whose mind, speech and body are quiescent and who have thoroughly concentrated their mind on meditation, it does not matter at all whether they stay in a densely populated habitation or in a secluded forest.

– *Dhyāna. 36*

Fire of Meditation

5. Just as fire fanned by powerful winds destroys heaps of firewood in no time so also the fire of meditation destroys heaps of karmas in a moment.

– Dhyāna. 101

Reflection of Soul

6. When the conscience is freed from sensual pleasures, the soul can be seen reflected in it.

– Bha. Ā.74

Thought Process

7. Meditation is perfected when the thought process becomes pure and sublime.

– Daśaśru. Sū.5.1

Absorbed in Meditation

8. A person whose mind is absorbed in meditation is not perturbed by miseries born of passions, nor those born of jealousy, dejection, grief and other mental anxieties.

– Dhyāna. 103

Contemplation of Self

9. To give up all fallacies and to be absorbed in the contemplation of the self is supreme Dharma Dhyāna.

– Kā. A. 482

Mind Control

10. The irresolute and fleeting mind, which is difficult to be controlled and conquered, becomes steadfast and tranquil by meditation.

– Ātma. 9

One Subject

11. To concentrate one's mind upon one subject is meditation.

– Āva. Ni. 1499

Kinds of Meditation

12. Of the four kinds of meditation, mournful (Ārta

Dhyāna) and wrathful (Raudra Dhyāna) cause birth and death in mundane existence. Righteous or analytic (Dharma Dhyāna) and purest (Śukla Dhyāna) are instrumental in emancipation.

– *Dhyāna. 5*

Significant Meditation

13. An aspirant engaged in spiritual contemplation should relinquish mournful (Ārta) and wrathful (Raudra) meditation and practise righteous (dharma) and purest (Śukla) meditation. The wise declare this as significant meditation.

– *Uttarā. Sū. 30.35*

53. Equanimity (Sāmāyika)

Equipoise

1. He who has no desire for mundane fulfilment and who refrains from all activities that cause karmic bondage is said to be equipoised.

– *Sū.Kṛ. Sū. 1.2.2.20*

Equanimity

2. Equanimity is to be devoid of attachment and aversion and to be indifferent in life and death, gain and loss, fortune and misfortune, friend and foe, joy and sorrow.

– *Mū. 23*

Oneness of Soul

3. The oneness of soul with right faith, knowledge, self-restraint and austerity is Samaya. Know this also as Sāmāyika.

– *Mū. 519*

Fruitless Sāmāyika

4. The Sāmāyika of a householder will be fruitless if he reflects upon mundane matters while practising Sāmāyika, as his concentration will become meaningless.

– *Sāvaya. 313*

Eliminate all Sins

5. The practice of Sāmāyika eliminates all sinful occupations.

– Uttarā. Sū. 29.9

54. Scriptural Study

None Equals Scriptural Study

1. Among the twelve internal and external austerities experienced by a wise person, there is none that equals or will be equal to the study of scriptures.

– Bha. Ā. 107

Freed from Miseries

2. By constantly studying the scriptures, one can be freed from all miseries.

– Uttarā. Sū. 26.10

Knowledge of All Subjects

3. The knowledge of all subjects is comprehended through the study of scriptures.

– Uttarā. Sū. 26.37

Knowledge-Obscuring Karmas

4. Knowledge-obscuring karmas are destroyed by the study of scriptures.

– Uttarā. Sū. 29.18

Knowledge of an Ignorant Person

5. Just as a blind person cannot delight in the presence of moonlight, so also the knowledge of an ignorant person, who studies the scriptures over and over, but is unable to experience the truth, is insignificant.

– Bṛ. Bhā. 1224

Types of Scriptural Studies

6. Study of scriptures (Svādhyāya) is of five types:
   Vācānā: careful and thorough study of scriptures.
   Pṛcchanā: clarification of the doubts aroused while studying the scriptures.
   Parivartanā: repeated recitation.

Anuprekṣā: reflection upon scriptural knowledge acquired.

Dharma-kathā: preaching of the doctrine.

– Uttarā. Sū. 30.34

Liberation

7. Just as a threaded needle when dropped carelessly is not lost but is easily traced, so also a person who has thorough understanding of scriptures may become imprudent for a while, but in no time makes amends and is finally liberated.

– Mū. 971

Benefits of Scriptural Study

8. Svādhyāya enables one to acquire knowledge of the well-being of the self, subjugate evil thoughts, become inclined towards renunciation, achieve tranquillity in thought, word and deed, practise austerity, and develop supreme disposition and benevolence.

– Bha. Ā. 100

□

XI
Precepts on Learning

55. Learning

The Deserving

1. He who always stays with the preceptor, who practises meditation and austerities, who has religious zeal and ardour for study, who is pleasant in action and speech deserves to be instructed.

– *Uttarā. Sū. 11.14*

Obstacles in Learning

2. Pride, anger, carelessness, illness and idleness are the five obstacles in the path of acquiring knowledge.

– *Uttarā. Sū. 11.3*

Worthy of Acquiring Knowledge

3. The eight factors that define a person as worthy of acquiring knowledge are: (a) not to indulge in ridiculous gossip, (b) not to lose control of the mind and the senses, (c) not to disclose secrets of others, (d) not to be undisciplined, (e) not to be blameworthy, (f) not to be covetous, (g) not to be short-tempered, (h) and not to forsake truth.

– *Uttarā. Sū. 11.4-5*

Scriptural Studies

4. By scriptural study, one acquires knowledge, has concentration of mind, is fixed in religion and helps others to be so fixed. Thus, by studying multifarious

sutras, he becomes absorbed in the contemplation of what is expounded therein.

– Daśa. Sū.9.4.3

Ācāryas

5. Just as a lamp lights hundreds of other lamps and yet remains lighted, so are the Ācāryās who enlighten others and remain enlightened themselves.

– Uttarā. Ni. 8

Noble Preceptor

6. A noble preceptor is one who imparts that knowledge and initiation by which the karmas are destroyed.

– Bo. Pā. 16

Initiation of the Aspirant

7. The initiation of the aspirant is fruitless if his actions do not synchronise with the knowledge acquired.

– Vya. Bhā. 7.215

56. Humility

Foundation of Faith

1. Humility is the foundation of Jaina faith. The practice of self-restraint and austerity should make one humble and modest. To a person who is not humble, righteousness and austerity are of no avail.

– Updeśa 1.341

Humble Disciple

2. Unlike a stubborn horse that waits for the express command of his master, a humble disciple – like a well-trained horse - does not wait but renounces the sinful activities by a mere hint from his preceptor.

– Uttarā. Sū. 1.12

Modest

3. He who is modest gains knowledge, and he who is arrogant, fails to gain it. Only he who knows these two axioms can be educated and enlightened.

– Daśa. Sū. 9.2.22

Roots of Fruits

4. From the roots of a tree, the shoots develop, and from shoots, the branches and twigs. Thereafter the leaves, flowers and fruits full of rich taste spring forth.

   – *Daśa. Sū. 9.2.1*

Humility

5. Likewise, humility is the root of righteousness (dharma) and emancipation the final object. With humility, a person learns the knowledge of scriptures quickly, gains eminence and finally gets liberated.

   – *Daśa. Sū. 9.2.2*

Learning with Humility

6. Learning tempered with humility is beneficial in this world and the next. Just as a plant cannot grow without water, learning will not be fruitful without humility.

   – *Bṛ. Bhā. 5203*

Discipline

7. A wise and fearless disciple benefits from the discipline imposed by the master for his own welfare, peace and self-purification while it evokes hatred in the ignorant disciple.

   – *Uttarā. Sū. 1.29*

Obedient

8. One who is obedient to the preceptor has heard the significance of religion and is equipped with humility traverses the difficult ocean of birth and death and attains emancipation.

   – *Daśa. Sū. 9.2.24*

Humility

9. Humility is austerity and austerity is dharma.

   – *Praśna. 2.3*

Not Humble

10. A person who is not humble should not be instructed about right conduct; of what use are ornaments for the person whose hands are mutilated?

    – *Bṛ. Bhā. 782*

57. Discretion

Ever Vigilant

1. An aspirant, ever vigilant – while he stands, sits, sleeps, eats and talks – is not bound by evil deeds.

– Daśa. Sū. 4.8

True Quest

2. My diligent pursuit in austerity, discipline, self-control, self-study, meditation and other obligatory duties is my true quest and journey.

– Bha. Sū. 19.207

Uncontaminated

3. If a Śramaṇa is vigilant in his conduct, he remains uncontaminated like the lotus in water.

– Pra. Sā. 3.18

58. Forbearance

Tolerance

1. A monk endures hunger, thirst, discomfort, cold, heat, fear and anguish with an unperturbed mind. Toleration of suffering caused to the body will entail him great benefits.

– Daśa. Sū. 8.27

All Creatures Suffer

2. 'It is not I alone who suffer but all creatures in the world too suffer'; thus a wise man should ruminate and patiently bear the afflictions that befall him, without giving way to his passions.

– Sū.Kṛ. Sū. 1.2.13

Being Impassive

3. Just as a mountain remains unmoved by the tempestuous winds, so also an aspirant who has taken vows should remain impassive to pleasant and unpleasant, great and small, favourable and unfavourable conditions.

– Sū.Kṛ. Sū. 1.11.37

Forbearance

4. Knowingly that all hardships and afflictions are a result of one's past deeds, ascetics bear them patiently like a debtor who strives to pay off his debts.

– Dvā. A. 110

Karmas are Powerful

5. Karmas are very powerful in this world and nothing is more powerful than karmas. Just as an elephant tramples a forest full of lotuses, so also when karmas are strong, they render all other powers weak.

– Bha. Ā. 1621

59. Restraint in Speech

Careful Speech

1. A wise person neither speaks without being asked nor does he interfere when another person is speaking. He doesnotspeakaboutsomebodyinhisabsenceandavoids deceitful untruth.

– Daśa. Sū. 8.47

Kinds of Speech

2. Speech is of four kinds – (a) true, (b) not true, (c) diluted, and (d) conventional speech.

– Daśa. Cū. 7.1

Speaking Wisely

3. A seeker should know these kinds of speeches and communicate either the truthful or the conventional. He should give up the false and diluted speech completely.

– Daśa. Sū. 7.1

Discerning Speech

4. A person with intellectual discrimination should not brand a blind person as blind, an eunuch so, a diseased and a thief likewise.

– Daśa. Sū. 7.12

Apt Speech

5. A wise ascetic should speak what he has seen; his speech should be brief, free from ambiguity and clearly expressed. His speech should neither be deceptive nor cause anxiety to anyone.

– Daśa. Sū. 8.39

Non-intrusion

6. One should not interrupt when the wise are seriously involved in scholarly discussions.

– Āva. Ni. 2.3.3.6

Harmful Speech

7. An aspirant should not utter words that may be harmful or cause displeasure or which may put another person out of form.

– Daśa. Sū. 8.48

Avoid Fraudulent Speech

8. A monk should not interrupt when two persons are engrossed in discussions. He should also not use trenchant and fraudulent speech and should answer only after due reflection.

– Sū.Kṛ. Sū. 1.9.25

Intention in Speech

9. That speech is right which purifies conduct, regardless of whether it is the truth or not. That speech is wrong which does not purify conduct, whether it is the truth or not. Verily, the seeker should watch his intention even more than his words.

– Daśa. Cū. 7

Reflected Speech

10. One should speak after due reflection. Just as a blind man needs the help of a guide to show him the path, speech also requires the guidance of the intellect.

– Vya. Bhā. 1513

Proper Speech

11. That speech is proper which is beneficial, moderate, measured and affable.

– Daśa. Ni. 322

60. Vigilance

Be Vigilant

1. Carelessness causes inflow of karma while vigilance averts it. He who is not vigilant is unwise and he who is vigilant is wise.

– Sū.Kṛ. Sū. 1.8.3

Vigilance and Fearlessness

2. A person who is not vigilant is faced with fear from all directions while there is no fear for a person who is vigilant.

– Ācā. Sū. 1.3.4.2

Inculcating Vigilance

3. Intoxication, merriment, passions, inertia and gossip – these five belong to the realm of non-vigilance; abstention from such negative traits is vigilance.

– Uttarā.Ni. 180

Stay Alert

4. The wise and prudent should remain alert even amidst the company of the idle and the indolent. Knowing that time is treacherous and the body is feeble, he should move about as watchfully as the bharanda bird (a mythological bird which has two heads and one body).

– Uttarā. Sū. 4.6

Hurdles

5. An indolent person can never be happy and a lethargic person can never acquire knowledge. A person with attachments cannot acquire renunciation and one who has a violent attitude cannot be compassionate.

– Ni. Bhā. 5307

Benefits of Vigilance

6. O man, always be vigilant. He who is vigilant gains more and more knowledge. He who is not vigilant is not blessed. Blessed is he who is always vigilant.

– Ṛṣi. 35.22

Immediacy

7. Do not procrastinate. What you have to do, do today itself, for lurking death may lay its cruel hands on you any moment.

– Bṛ. Bhā. 4674

Do Not Postpone

8. Follow the path of righteousness and waste not a single moment. Life is full of obstacles and so one should not postpone anything for tomorrow.

– Bṛ. Bhā. 4675

Present Moment

9. Use the present moment most purposefully.

– Sū.Kṛ. Sū. 1.2.3.19

Wisdom

10. One should acquire meaningful knowledge and avoid what is meaningless.

– Uttarā. Sū. 1.8

Vigilance and Karma

11. Just as fire burns dry wood in no time, so also an ever-vigilant aspirant absorbed in the contemplation of the self, destroys the heap of karmas in no time.

– Ācā. Sū. 1.4.3.33

Wakefulness

12. Imperfect is the knowledge of a person who is not vigilant and perfect is the knowledge of a person who is ever wakeful and vigilant.

– Bṛ. Bhā. 3384

61. Fearlessness

Effect of Fear

1. A timid person is always helpless and, under the influence of some fear or the other, makes others also fearful. Such a person is influenced by evil spirits.

– Praśna. 2.2

Outcome of Fear

2. One who is fearful gives up the practice of austerity and self-restraint. He is unable to shoulder any important responsibility and becomes incompetent to tread the path of righteousness.

– Praśna.2.2

Conquering Fear

3. One should conquer all kinds of fears – fear of sudden calamities, dreadful diseases, tensions, old age and even the fear of death.

– Praśna.2.2

Abhayadāna

4. To protect all living beings who fear death is the highest form of charity (abhayadāna); this is supreme among all charities.

– Vasu. Śra. 338

Devotion to Jaina

5. A person who has firm devotion towards Jaina like the steady mountain Meru, has inclination for renunciation and is free from defects of character will have no fear in this world.

– Bha. Ā. 745

Causes of Fear

6. The seven causes of fear are: 1. Fear related to the present birth, 2. Fear related to the next birth, 3. Fear of movements, 4. Fear of sudden calamities, 5. Fear of livelihood, 6. Fear of death, and 7. Fear of disrepute.

– Shtā. Sū. 7.27

Move Fearlessly

7. An aspirant should always move about fearlessly.

– Ni. Bhā. 273

62. Food Regimen

Shun Rich Food

1. One should shun rich food in excess for they stimulate the passions. A passionate person is always attracted by the sensual desires just as a bird is attracted by a tree laden with ripe fruits.

– Uttarā. Sū. 32.10

Avoid Excessive Food

2. As in a dense forest, a fire fanned by strong winds cannot be extinguished, so also the sensual fire (as it were) of the person who eats food in excessive quantity can never be extinguished. Therefore, excessive food is not beneficial for a celibate.

– Uttarā. Sū. 32.11

Restricted Diet

3. Noble aspirants do not consume food for taste or pleasure; they regulate their diet solely for religious pursuits.

– Mū. 810

Unfavourable Food

4. Excessively spicy and flavoured food is instant poison for an aspirant who seeks enlightenment.

– Uttarā. Sū. 16.12.13

Flavoured Food

5. Excessive spicy food excites the passions.

– Āva. Ni.1280

Own Physician

6. Those who take wholesome and healthy food in small quantities never fall sick and do not need the services of a physician. They are their own physicians.

– O. Ni. 578

Regulated Diet

7. Knowledge is instrumental in emancipation and the body is instrumental in the acquisition of knowledge. Hence, an aspirant is permitted to take regulated diet for the sustenance of the body.

– Ni. Bhā. 4159

Eat Before Sunset

8. Intake of food after sunset is prohibited.

– Uttarā. Sū. 19.31

Minimal Food

9. To eat minimal food is always beneficial.

– Ni. Bhā. 2951

63. Company of the Virtuous

Beneficial Company

1. Company of the virtuous progressively promotes scriptural study, knowledge (especially higher knowledge), detachment, self-restraint, stoppage of karmic influx, austerities, annihilation of previously acquired karmas, state of inaction and final emancipation.

– Bha. Sū. 2.111

Company of Virtuous

2. A person in solitude is subject to all kinds of doubts and uncertainties every moment. Hence, the company of the holy and virtuous should be sought.

– Bṛ. Bhā. 5719

Wrong Association

3. Just as water loses its inherent nature on contact with fire, so also the pious abandon their virtues when they associate themselves with the wicked.

– Bha. Ā. 344

Kind of Company

4. Just as water in the earthen jar becomes aromatic

when in contact with the fragrant lotus, but tepid and tasteless when in contact with fire, so also the company of the pious enhances one's wisdom and the company of the wicked distorts one's understanding.

– Mū. 954

The Right Company

5. Knowing righteousness and non-violence in its entirety, the equanimous and restrained aspirant should always seek the company of the wise.

– Ṛṣi. 33.17

Wrong Company

6. The reputation of a noble person gets tarnished in the company of wicked people just as a fragrant garland becomes worthless when offered to a dead body.

– Bha. Ā. 345

64. Noble Conduct

Wise Behaviour

1. Always be calm, do not speak excessively, and learn meaningful verses in the presence of the wise. Leave aside whatever is worthless.

– Uttarā. Sū. 1.8

Discipline

2. The wise should not shun discipline. They must adorn forgiveness and avoid the company of the mean-minded, and not indulge in frivolousness.

– Uttarā. Sū. 1.9

Talk Less

3. Talk less, never speak when resentful, study the scriptures regularly and then meditate upon the true nature of the self.

– Uttarā. Sū. 1.10

Respecting the Wise

4. Do not be discourteous to the wise, neither in speech nor deed; neither openly nor covertly.

   – *Uttarā. Sū. 1.17*

Prescribed Conduct

5. He who adheres to the prescribed and approved conduct practised by the knowledgeable incurs no criticism.

   – *Uttarā. Sū. 1.42*

□

XII
Other Precepts

65. The Four

Types of Men

1. There are four types of men – some abandon the guise of a monk but not righteousness; some give up the conduct but not the appearance of a monk; some forsake both while others renounce neither.

– Vya. Sū. 10

Types of Sons

2. There are four types of sons – some are more virtuous than their fathers; some are evenly matched with their fathers; while some are more worthless than their fathers; and some are so lacking in character that they bring disgrace to the family.

– Sthā. Sū. 4.1

Types of Meetings

3. Meetings are of four kinds – with some an encounter may be pleasant but their company may not be good; while with some others, an encounter may not be pleasant but their company may be enriching. However, with some, the encounter as well as their company is rewarding; while with some others, the encounter as well as their company is harmful.

– Sthā. Sū. 4.1

Base Instincts

4. Deception, fraud, lies and malpractices in trade – these are the four base instincts which drag the soul to sub-human existence.

– Sthā. Sū. 4.4

Four Virtues

5. Simplicity, humility, compassion and serenity – these are the four virtues that enable the soul to acquire human birth.

– Sthā. Sū. 4.4.630

The Unworthy

6. Four types of people are not worthy of acquiring scriptural knowledge – the vain, the greedy, the quarrelsome and the deceitful.

– Sthā. Sū. 4.3.452

Types of Clouds

7. Four types of clouds can be seen – those that thunder but do not rain; those which are rain-bearing but do not thunder; those that thunder as well as rain; and those that neither thunder nor rain.

– Sthā. Sū. 4.4

Kinds of Philanthropists

8. Like the clouds, philanthropists are also of four kinds – some talk proudly of donating but do not donate; some donate liberally but do not utter a word about it; some donate as well as indulge in self-praise; while some others neither speak nor donate.

– Sthā. Sū. 4.4.533

66. Some Significant Illustrations

Repentance by the Ignorant

1. As a cart driver who intentionally leaves the smooth highway and gets on a rugged road repents when the axle breaks, so the ignorant one, who transgresses the

path of righteousness and embraces unrighteousness, repents at the time of his death over the broken axle of his life.

– Uttarā. Sū. 5.14.15

Dharma in Practical Life

2. Three merchants went abroad with capital to earn money; one of them earned good profit while the second retained his capital but the third one lost his entire capital. This is an example taken from common life. This applies to Dharma as well.

– Uttarā. Sū. 7.14,15

Ill-Natured

3. Just as a bitch with ulcerous ear is driven away from everywhere, so also the ill-natured, insubordinate and talkative disciple is expelled disgracefully wherever he goes.

– Uttarā. Sū. 1.4

Characterless Person

4. However much milk a snake may drink, it is unable to give up its poisonous nature; so also a characterless person, who may study innumerable scriptures, remains unable to shed his wicked nature.

– Sa.Sā. 317

Sinning Secretly

5. A person who drinks poison secretly surely succumbs to death; so also a person who sins in secret definitely gets corrupted.

– Sū.Kṛ. Ni. 52

67. Some More Aphorisms

Genuine Ascetic

1. He who can objectively evaluate his inner self is a genuine ascetic (Nirgrantha).

– Ācā. Sū. 2.15

Do not Scorn

2. He who scorns others wanders aimlessly in the cycle of births.

– Sū.Kṛ. Sū. 1.2.2.2

The Present

3. The present moment is important, strive to make it fruitful.

– Sū.Kṛ. Sū. 1.2.3.19

Meaningless Gestures

4. If by bathing regularly one can attain perfection, then the marine creatures must have attained perfection long ago.

– Sū.Kṛ. Sū. 1.7.14

Trustworthiness

5. A monk hears and sees many things but it is not proper to reveal them in public.

– Daśa. Sū. 8.20

Enlightenment

6. It is not possible to get enlightenment again and again.

– Daśa. Cū. 1.14

Relinquish the Meaningless

7. Absorb the meaningful and relinquish the meaningless.

– Uttarā. Sū. 1.8

Care of the Body

8. One should take care of this body so as only to reduce the accumulated karmic bondage.

– Uttarā. Sū. 6.14

Mere Study

9. Mere study of sacred texts cannot protect anyone.

– Uttarā. Sū. 14.12

Axis of Righteousness

10. Not wealth but nobility of conduct is necessary for moving the axis of dharma.

– Uttarā. Sū. 14.17

Service to Others

11. By service one acquires the meritorious karmas which bring about for him the form (Nāma) and status (Gotra) of a Tīrthaṇkara.

– Uttarā. Sū. 29.43

Gambling

12. A blind person is able to apprehend various things through all senses other than the eyes. But a gambler is unable to apprehend anything, though he possesses all the senses.

– Vasu. Śrā. 66

Courageous

13. No task daunts the courageous.

– Bṛ. Bhā. 1357

Idle Person

14. An idle and inactive person finds fault with everything and everyone, not withstanding his own shortcomings.

– Bṛ. Bhā. 2138

Real Ornaments

15. The real ornaments that enhance the beauty of a woman are chastity and modesty; the others are mere appendages.

– Bṛ. Bhā. 4118

Miserable

16. Miserable is not he who dies while seeking self-realisation, but miserable is he who gives up self-restraint, becomes perverted and leads an aimless life.

– Ni. Bhā. 1717

Sustenance

17. Knowledge is instrumental for emancipation and the body is instrumental for acquisition of knowledge. Hence, an aspirant is permitted to take regulated diet for the sustenance of the body.

– Bṛ. Bhā. 5281

Hunger

18. There is no greater suffering than hunger.

– Pinda. Ni. 663

Mere Pretension

19. By retiring to the forest alone if one can become wise and austere, then the lions, leopards and other denizens of the forest can become so.

– Ācā. Cū. 1.7.1

Self-Knowledge

20. What other fortune do the saints require after having acquired the sublime treasure of self-knowledge?

– Sū.Kṛ. Cū. 1.14

Mere Knowledge

21. Knowledge alone does not enable a task to be accomplished.

– Ācā. Ni. 1156

Reviling Others

22. The wicked makes light of his major faults but invariably blows out of proportion even the minor faults of others.

– Uttarā. Ni. 140

Emancipation

23. Despite strict observation of vows and rigorous austerities, one can never attain emancipation without self-realisation.

– Sa. Sā. 153

Unwise Reflections

24. Ignorant is he who thinks that he makes others sad or happy; the wise do not reflect thus.

– Sa. Sā. 253

Timeliness

25. Those who exert themselves at the proper time feel no remorse afterwards.

– Sū.Kṛ. Sū. 1.3.4

Secrecy

26. One should not reveal the secrets of others.

– Sū.Kṛ. Sū. 1.9.26

Presence of Master

27. Sunrise can be visualised only when one has vision. Truth can be realised only in the presence of the master.

– Sū.Kṛ. Sū. 1.14.13

Dharma's Abode

28. Populous town, village or forest has no relevance to the practice of dharma as it is the self in which it abides.

– Ācā. Sū. 1.8.1

Scriptures and Knowledge

29. Scriptures are not knowledge in themselves because they don't know anything by themselves. Therefore, scriptures are different from knowledge.

– Sa.Sā. 390

Observing Vows

30. Whether a monk or a householder, he who sincerely observes the vows definitely acquires a noble birth. He who is unrighteous is bound to go to hell.

– Uttarā. Sū. 5.22

Company of Scholar

31. Just as no one seeks shelter under a tree surrounded by thorny creepers although laden with sweet fruits, so also none prefers the company of a scholar who abuses and talks ill of others.

– Bṛ. Bhā. 6092

Mankind

32. Mankind is one.

– Ācā. Ni. 19

68. The Last Sermon

Withering Leaves

1. O Gautama, just as the dry leaves of a tree wither away, so also human life comes to an end when the duration of life terminates. Therefore, be not careless even for a while.

– *Uttarā. Sū. 10.1*

Vanishing Dew Drops

2. O Gautama, as dew drops last but for a while on the Kuśa grass tips (a species of grass), so is the life of man. Therefore, be not careless even for a while.

– *Uttarā. Sū. 10.2*

Precious Life

3. It is indeed very difficult to acquire human birth. One acquires it after a very long span of time for the karmas that bind the soul are very powerful. Therefore, O Gautama, be not carless even for a while.

– *Uttarā. Sū. 10.4*

Like the Lotus

4. Just as the lotus remains unaffected by the autumnal water, you too should give up all attachments. O Gautama, be not careless even for a while.

– *Uttarā. Sū. 10.28*

Crossing Over

5. O Gautama, when you have crossed the mighty ocean, why tarry near the shore? Hurry to go across, be not careless even for a while.

– *Uttarā. Sū. 10.34*

Weakening Body

6. O Gautama, your body has become feeble, your hair has become grey and all your strength is depleted. Therefore, be not careless even for a while.

– *Uttarā. Sū. 10.26*

Path of Peace

7. O Gautama, whether in a village or in a city, steadily proceed on the path of peace by restraint and enlightenment. Be not careless even for a while.

– Uttarā. Sū. 10.36

69. Essence of Jaina Dharma

Jaina Dharma

1. What you desire for yourself, desire for others too; what you do not desire for yourself, do not at all desire for others – this is the essence of Jaina dharma.

– Bṛ. Bhā. 4584

Essence of Teachings

2. The essence of preaching is practice and the fruit of practice is emancipation.

– Ācā. Ni. 17

Essence of Scriptures

3. What is the essence of scriptures? It is right conduct.

– Ācā. Ni. 16

□

Abbreviations of the Selected Works

Adh. Sā.	:	Adhyātma-sāra
Amit. Śra.	:	Amitagati Śrāvakācāra
Arh. Pra.	:	Arhat Pravacana
Aupa. Sū.	:	Aupapātika Sūtra
Ācā. Cū.	:	Ācārāṅga Cūrṇi
Ācā. Ni.	:	Ācārāṅga Niryukti
Ācā. Sū.	:	Ācārāṅga Sūtra
Ātma.	:	Ātmāvabodhakulakaṁ
Ātur. Pra.	:	Āturpratyākhyāna
Āva. Cū.	:	Āvaśyaka Cūrṇi
Āva. Ni.	:	Āvaśyaka Niryukti
Āva. Sū.	:	Āvaśyaka Sūtra
Bha. Ā.	:	Bhagavatī Ārādhanā
Bha. Pa.	:	Bhakta-parijña
Bha. Sū.	:	Bhagavati Sūtra
Bhā. Pā.	:	Bhāva Pāhuḍa
Bo. Pā.	:	Bodha-Pāhuda
Bṛ. Bhā.	:	Bṛhatkalpa Bhāṣya
Dar. Pā.	:	Darśana-Pāhuda
Daśa. Cū.	:	Daśavaikālika-Cūrṇi
Daśa. Cūl.	:	Daśavaikālika-Cūlikā
Daśa. Ni.	:	Daśavaikālika-Niryukti
Daś. Sū.	:	Daśavaikālika-Sūtra
Daśaśru. Sū.	:	Daśaśrutaskandha-Sūtra
Dhyāna.	:	Dhyāna Śataka

Dravya.	:	Dravya-Saṅgraha
Dvā. A.	:	Dvādaśānuprekṣā
Jñātā.	:	Jñātādharmakathā
Kalpa. Sū.	:	Kalpa-Sūtra
Kā. A.	:	Kārtikeyānuprekṣā
Kām. Kath	:	Kāmaghata Kathānaka
Ku. A.	:	Kundakunda Anuprekṣā
Ku. Śra.	:	Kundakunda Śrāvakācāra
Ma. Pra.	:	Mahāpratyakhyāna Prakīrṇaka
Ma. Sa.	:	Maraṇsamādhi Prakīrṇaka
Mo. Pā.	:	Mokṣa Pāhuda
Mū.	:	Mūlācāra
Nandī.	:	Nandī-Sūtra
Naya.	:	Nayacakra
Ni. Bhā.	:	Niśītha Bhāṣhya
Ni. Cū.	:	Niśītha Cūrṇi
Ni. Sā.	:	Niyama Sāra
O. Ni	:	Ogha niryukti
Pañca.	:	Pañcāstikāya
Piṇḍa.	:	Piṇḍa-niryukti
Praśna.	:	Praśna-vyākaraṇa-Sūtra
Pra. Sā.	:	Pravacana-Sāra
Ra. Sā.	:	Rayaṇa-Sāra
Rāja.	:	Rājavārttika
Ṛṣi.	:	Ṛṣibhāṣita
Sa. Sā.	:	Samaya Sāra
Sa. Sū.	:	Samaṇa-Suttaṁ
Sama. Sū.	:	Samavāyaṅga Sūtra
Savaya.	:	Sāvayapaṇṇatti
Sī. Pā.	:	Sīla-Pāhuda
Sthā. Sū.	:	Sthānāṅga-Sūtra
Sū. Kṛ.Cū.	:	Sūtrakṛtāṅga Cūrṇi
Sū. Kṛ. Ni	:	Sūtrakṛtāṅga Niryukti

Sū. Kṛ. Sū.	:	Sūtrakṛtāṅga Sūtra
Sū. Pā.	:	Sūtra-Pāhuda
Ta. Sā.	:	Tattva-Sāra
Updeśa	:	Updeśamālā
Upā. Sū.	:	Upāsakadaśāṅga Sūtra
Utta. Cū.	:	Uttarādhyayana Cūrṇi
Utta. Ni.	:	Uttarādhyayana Niryukti
Utta. Sū.	:	Uttarādhyayana Sūtra
Vasu. Śrā.	:	Vasunandi Śrāvakācāra
Vi. Bhā.	:	Viśeṣāvaśyaka Bhāṣhya
Vya. Bhā.	:	Vyavahāra-bhāṣya Pīṭhikā
Vya. Sū.	:	Vyavahāra-Sūtra

□□□

* 9 7 8 9 3 5 2 6 6 6 2 6 3 *
MAN - #0698 - 230726 - C0 - 216/140/8 - PB - 9789352666263 - Matt Lamination